My Big Fun Kindergarten Workbook with Handwriting

Learn to Read

100 Sight Words and Math Activities

We create our workbooks with love and great care.
For any issues with your workbook, such as printing errors, typos, faulty binding, or something
else, please do not hesitate to contact us at: info@homerunpress.com.
We will make sure you get a replacement copy immediately.

THANK YOU!

First published in the USA 2020.   ISBN 9781952368295

A is for alligator

A A A A A A A A

a a a a a a a a

ant ant

apple apple

B is for bird

B B B B B B

b b b b b b b

bird bird

boy boy

C is for cake

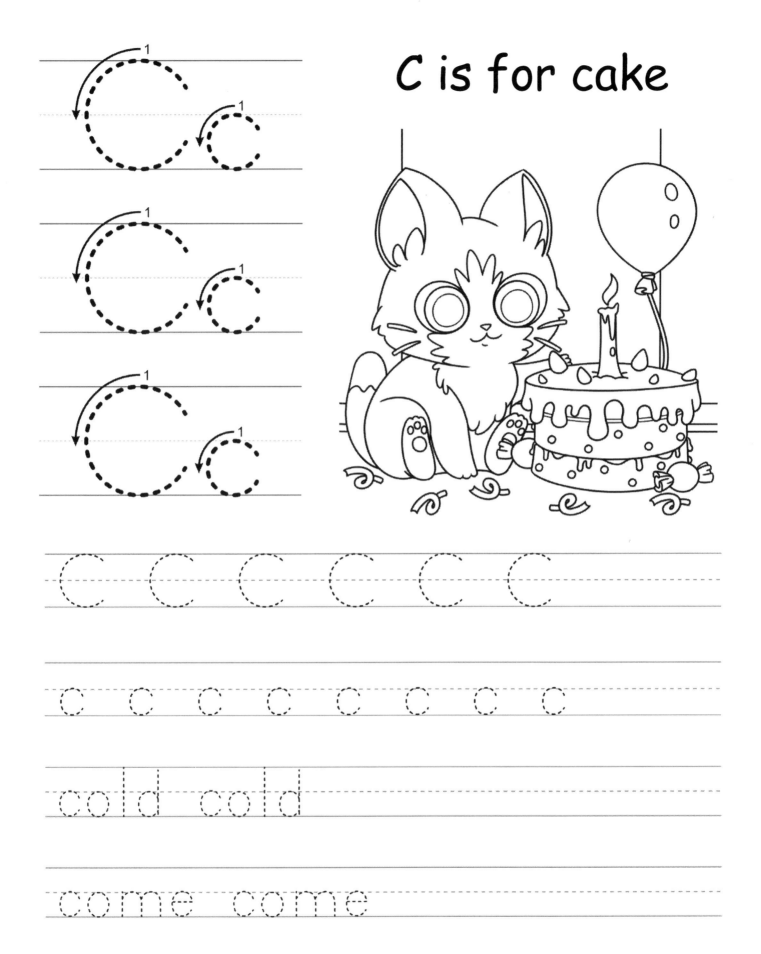

C C C C C C

c c c c c c c c

cold cold

come come

D is for dragon

E is for eagle

F is for fish

fish fish

flower flower

G is for giraffe

H is for horse

H H H H H H H

h h h h h h h

home home

hot hot

I is for island

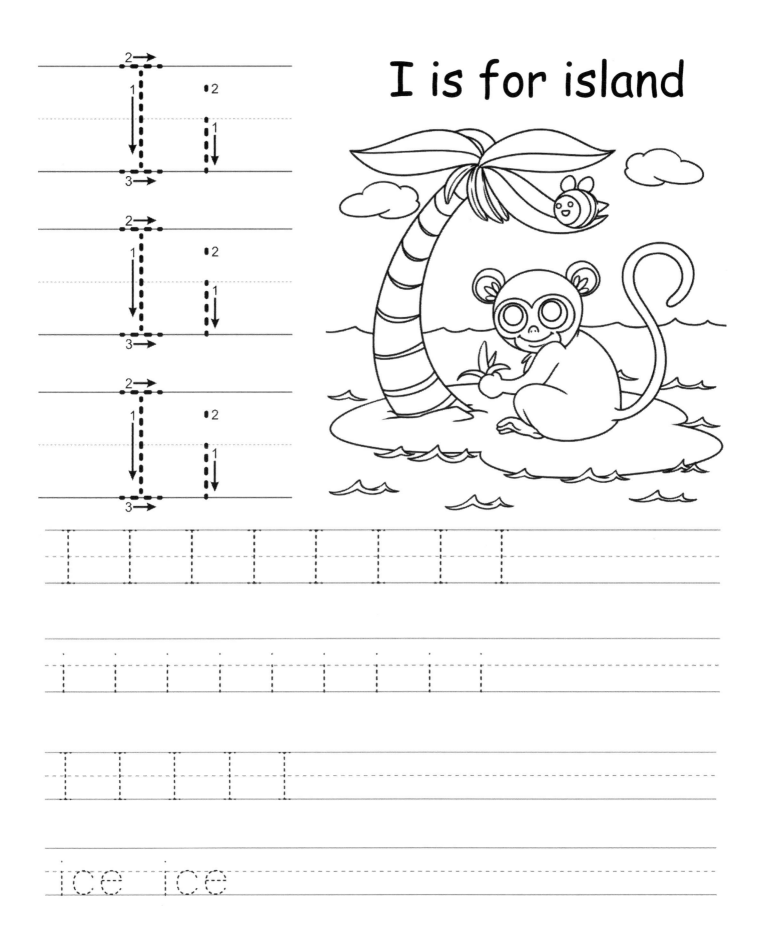

ice ice

J is for jam

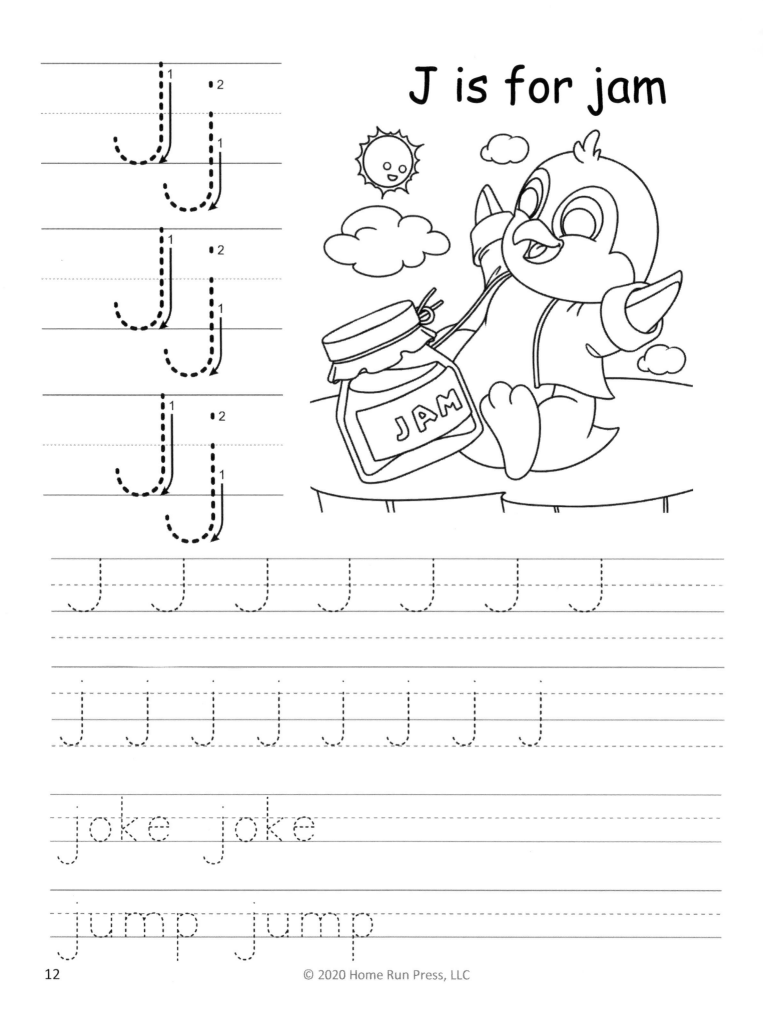

joke joke

jump jump

K is for key

K K K K K K

k k k k k k k

key key

kite kite

L is for lemon

leave leave

little little

M is for monkey

M M M M M M M M M

m m m m m m m m m

mother mother

milk milk

N is for nut

O is for owl

open open

our our

P is for pig

P P P P P P P

p p p p p p p

puppy puppy

put put

Q is for question

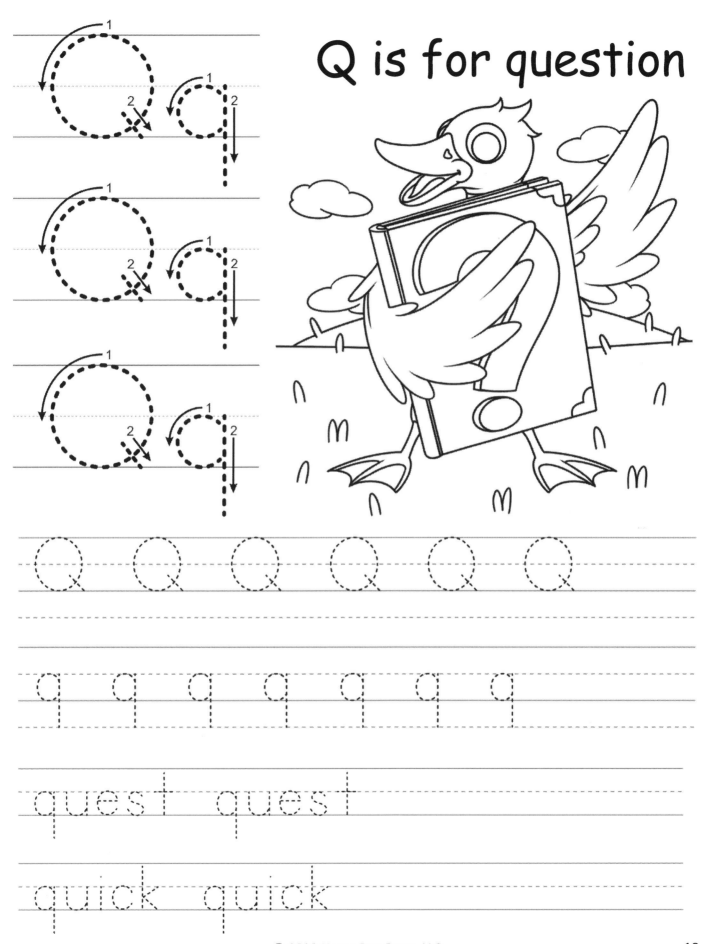

quest quest

quick quick

R is for rabbit

R R R R R R

r r r r r r r

read read

run run

S is for snake 6

T is for tree

3

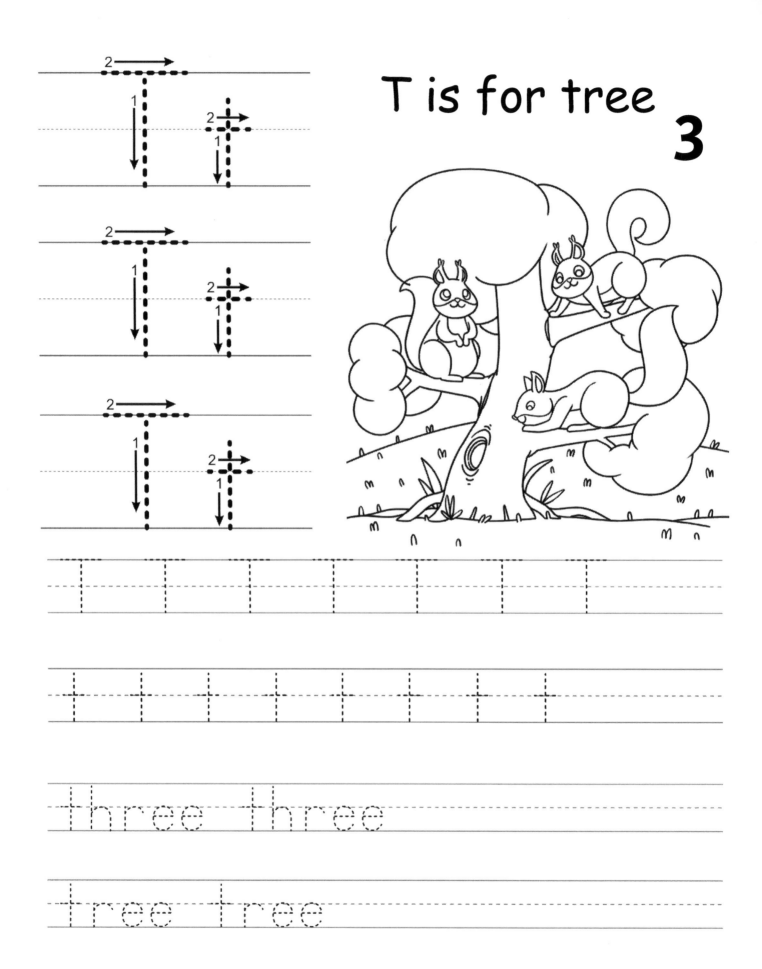

three three

tree tree

U is for unicorn

U U U U U U U U

u u u u u u u u u

ugly ugly

upper upper

V is for violin

van van

verb verb

W is for worm

X is for xylophone

Xmas

xylophone

Y is for yacht

Y Y Y Y Y Y Y Y

y y y y y y y y

yoga yoga

you you

Z is for zebra

zero zero

zebra zebra

Say the word. Trace the word. Write the word.

am am

are are

and and

ask ask

Read each sentence. Write the missing word (**"am"** or **"are"**).

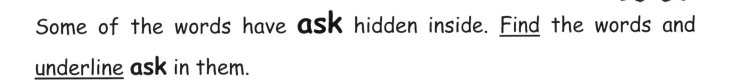

Racoons ___ always hungry.

I ___ happy to see you.

Some of the words have **ask** hidden inside. Find the words and underline **ask** in them.

task   basket   mask

Alaska   master   masque   land

Say the word. Trace the word. Write the word.

black black

brown brown

Read each sentence. Write the missing word ("black" or "brown").

Pandas are _____ and white bears.

Most monkeys are _____.

Here are some words that start with letter **C**. Say them aloud. Then trace each word.

can

come

could

can

come

could

Say the word. Trace the word. Write the word.

be be

but but

Read the words. Look and think about how they are related. Find the word that does not belong and circle it.

carrot

a) peach   b) cabbage   c) onion

fish

a) frog   b) snake   c) zebra

doctor

a) artist   b) mail   c) farmer

truck

a) ship   b) bus   c) car

Say the word. Trace the word. Write the word.

day day

eat eat

first first

Read each sentence. Write the missing word ("day" or "eat").

Lions like to spend the _____ under a tree. When the sun goes down, they _____.

Read each sentence. Write the missing word ("first").

One is the _____ number.

This is my _____ cupcake.

When I eat, I _____ wash my hands.

Say the word. Trace the word. Write the word.

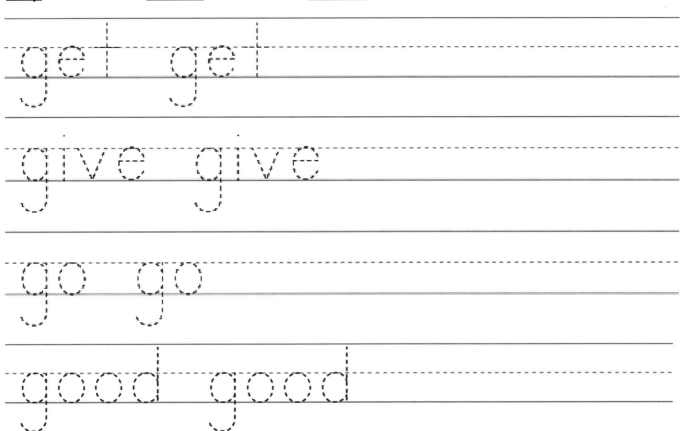

get get

give give

go go

good good

Find each word in the word search.

ARE   CAN   COME   DAY   BLACK

BROWN   FIRST   GET   GOOD

Q Q W X Z Y G X F X O J
V C F G Y S U I P F Q E
X X S N W O R B D O G C
P E U W A S C L A R E C
V T E C T C L D Y M T M
Z P U O W A D O O G K F
R L Z F X N K C A L B O

Say the word. Trace the word. Write the word.

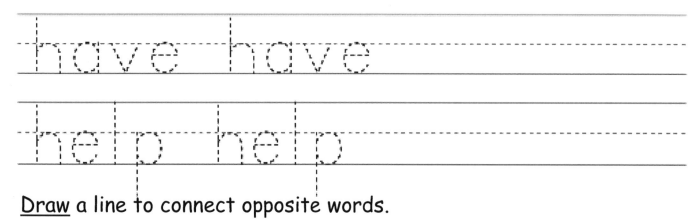

Draw a line to connect opposite words.

Antonyms are words that have opposite meanings.

new	throw
easy	boring
clean	sick
bright	rainy
sunny	dark
catch	old
funny	hard
well	dirty

Add each beginning letter or letters to the word ending to write new words.

 _and

 _ame

l_____

s_____

h_____

b_____

w_____

br_____

st_____

isl_____

n_____

f_____

c_____

g_____

s_____

bec_____

bl_____

sh_____

Say the word. Trace the word. Write the word.

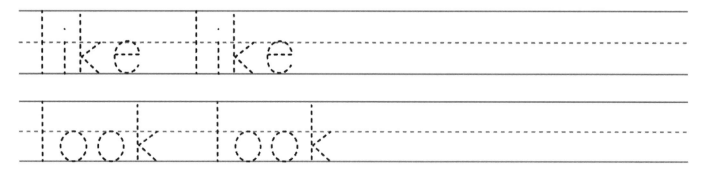

Draw a line to connect words that are the **same or synonyms**. Say the words.

Synonyms are words that mean exactly or almost the same.

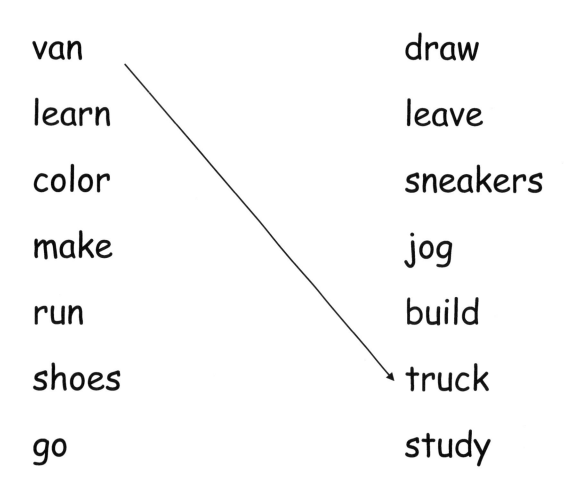

van	draw
learn	leave
color	sneakers
make	jog
run	build
shoes	truck
go	study

Say the word. Trace the word. Write the word.

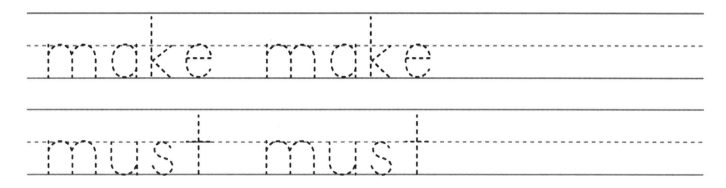

make make

must must

Draw a line to connect words that **rhyme**. Say the words.

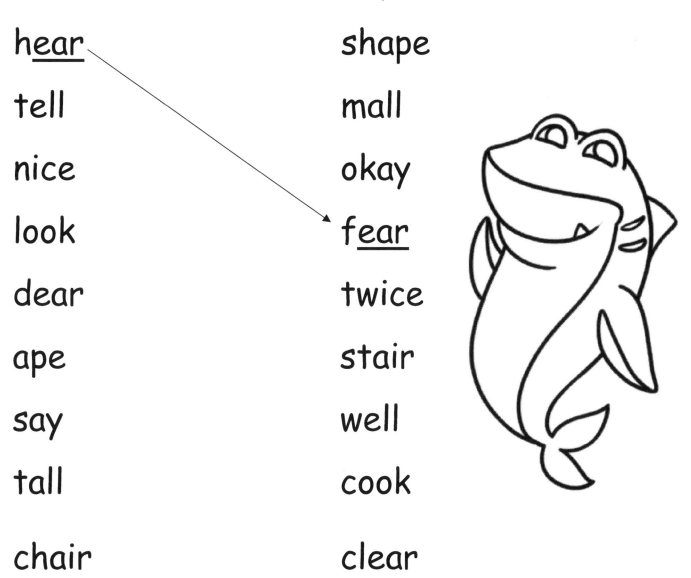

hear   shape

tell   mall

nice   okay

look   fear

dear   twice

ape   stair

say   well

tall   cook

chair   clear

Say the word. Trace the word. Write the word.

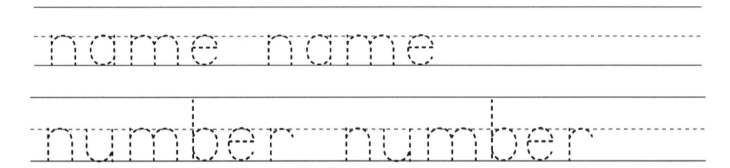

name name

number number

2. Draw a line from the snail to the pear with the letters that finish the word.

Add each beginning letter or letters to the word ending to write new words.

 _ar

 _ir

j_____

a_____

f_____

f_____

w_____

fa_____

ne_____

ha_____

he_____

cha_____

fe_____

pa_____

de_____

the_____

we_____

he_____

Say the word. Trace the word. Write the word.

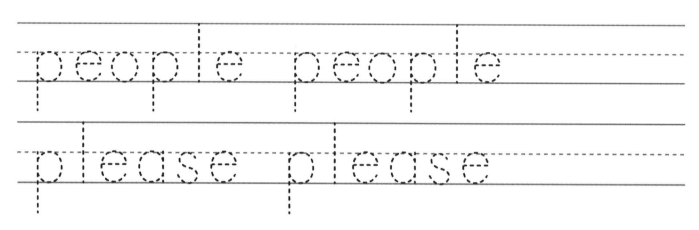

Read the words. Write the missing letters to write the word from the Choice Box.

old   play   out   must   help

part   have   people   please

h__lp

____ve

p__rt

o__d

pl____se

o__t

____ust

pl____

p__o__e

© 2020 Home Run Press, LLC

Say the word. Trace the word. Write the word.

read read

ride ride

Look at each box. Find the words whose letters fit in the boxes.
Write the words.

green   must   animal   number

black   purple   square   triangle

Say the word. Trace the word. Write the word.

she she

some some

Use the words from the Choice Box to unscramble the words below.

about   all   after   again   build

always   ask   blue   buy   before

forebe _____   kas _____

fater _____   lal _____

outba _____   belu _____

salway _____   aagin _____

dilub _____   uby _____

Write the words in the puzzle. Use the Choice Box to help you.

apple   lemon   pear   candy   pineapple

strawberry   cupcake   watermelon

Down

1. _ _ _ _ _ _ _ _ _ _

5. _ _ _ _ _

8. _ _ _ _ _

Across

2. _ _ _ _ _ _ _ _ _

3. _ _ _ _

4. _ _ _ _ _

6. _ _ _ _ _ _ _

7. _ _ _ _ _ _ _ _ _ _

Say the word. Trace the word. Write the word.

sad sad

see see

Draw a line to finish the sentences.

All living things need air   big clouds.

Hail is really frozen   air.

A windmill needs a power of   to live.

Hurricanes begin over the   land.

Tornadoes begin over   rain.

Snow is made of water and   ocean.

Thunderstorms are caused by   the wind.

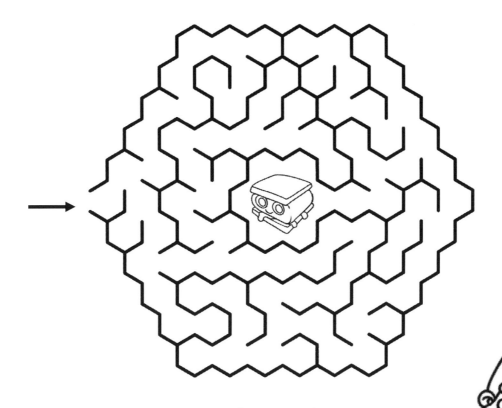

Find and circle or cross out the words.

```
F  B  T  K  F  G  O  D  H  P
J  B  C  O  K  B  L  F  F  A
Q  O  U  W  P  I  I  B  P  C
S  X  Z  B  R  F  T  E  L  B
V  K  Y  P  B  P  N  Q  D  I
Z  U  I  N  Y  L  F  B  Z  G
E  G  R  I  G  O  G  F  C  K
M  O  P  A  X  O  R  O  C  K
D  A  Z  R  I  N  F  E  Z  G
T  S  Y  T  Z  N  O  Z  N  G
```

BOX	FOX
DOG	FOG
CAP	TAP
SOCK	ROCK
MOP	TOP
BIG	PIG
RAIN	TRAIN

Say the word. Trace the word. Write the word.

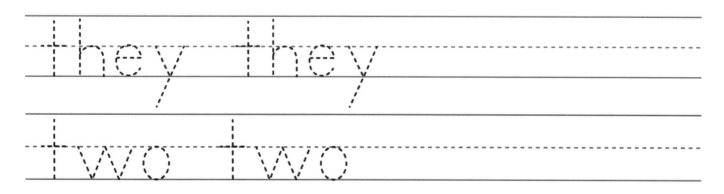

they they

two two

Color the lemons with the word inside.

than – red   money – blue

time – green   tree – yellow

mail – pink   train - brown

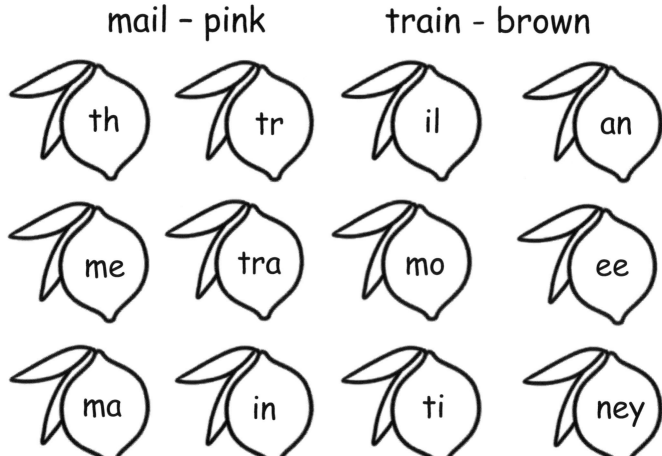

Say the word. Trace the word. Write the word.

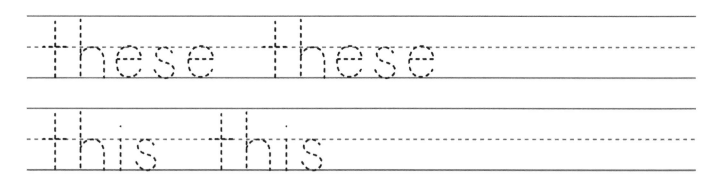

Read the words. Look and think about how they are related. Find the word that does not belong and circle it.

large

a) big   b) small   c) huge

library

a) school   b) house   c) cafe

hospital

a) playground b) post office c) library

boat

a) ship   b) tanker   c) tractor

Say the word. Trace the word. Write the word.

than than

Each word below is written in a secret code. Replace each letter in the words with the letter that comes **after** it in the alphabet. Write the words.

eqhdmc   _____

ehqrs   _____

fqnv   _____

bghkc   _____

bntkc   _____

annj   _____

lnqd   _____

Say the word. Trace the word. Write the word.

use use

want want

A *verb* is a word that *shows action*.

Circle the **verb** in each sentence.

Flowers (have) seeds inside them.

Dirt is made of very small pieces of rock.

Many kinds of animals live in forests.

Waves form at sea as winds blow.

River water comes from rainwater.

Icebergs are large mountains of ice.

Mountains are made from rock.

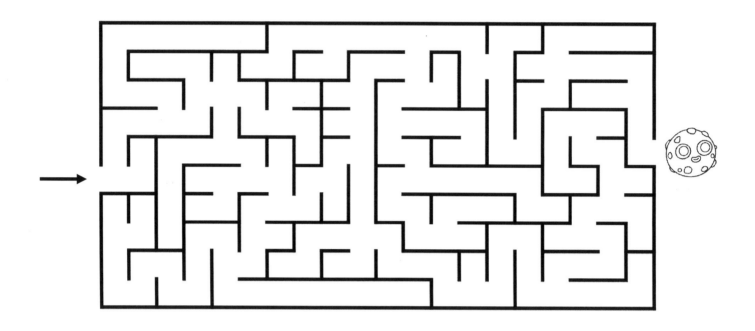

Find and circle or cross out the words.

E A D L P L R O Y O
X H A V X I I Q U R
W S S P G O N E E R
P C Y H I K M D Z Q
O L T P E O P L E K
T W E Y S T E E C X
H F N A A E R D X E
E N U R S L W I O A
R T R A P E P R L W
O I F X Y T D N D Z

ONE   OTHER

OUR   OLD

PART   PEOPLE

PLAY   PLEASE

RED   RIGHT

RUN   SHE

SAD   RIDE

SOME   SEE

Say the word. Trace the word. Write the word.

what what

when when

Unscramble and complete each sentence.

Rocks are _____ of minerals.
emad

Minerals _____ different shapes and
heav

_____.
crolos

Lava is melted _____. It _____
kocr   cemos
out from the center of the _____.
earht
Hot gases inside the _____ push the
tearh
_____ out.
vala

Write the words in the puzzle. Use the Choice Box to help you.

| clean | night | tree | key | flag |
| snow | road | please | river | cloud |

Across

2. opposite of day

4. magic word

6. a mass of water vapor in the sky

7. a highway

8. opens locks

Down

1. used as a symbol of a country

3. a woody plant

5. frozen rain

6. opposite of dirty

7. a large stream of water

Say the word. Trace the word. Write the word.

which   which

white   white

2. Rewrite the words in **alphabetical order**.

forest   1. _____

ant   2. _____

brother   3. _____

bee   4. _____

water   5. _____

saw   6. _____

toy   7. _____

get   8. _____

come   9. _____

Say the word. Trace the word. Write the word.

well well

Each word below is written in a secret code. Replace each letter in the words with the letter that comes **before** it in the alphabet. Write the words.

qmfbtf _____

upebz _____

nvtu _____

esbx _____

mpoh _____

mfgu _____

sjhiu _____

Draw a line to match the first syllable of each word to the second syllable. Write the words below.

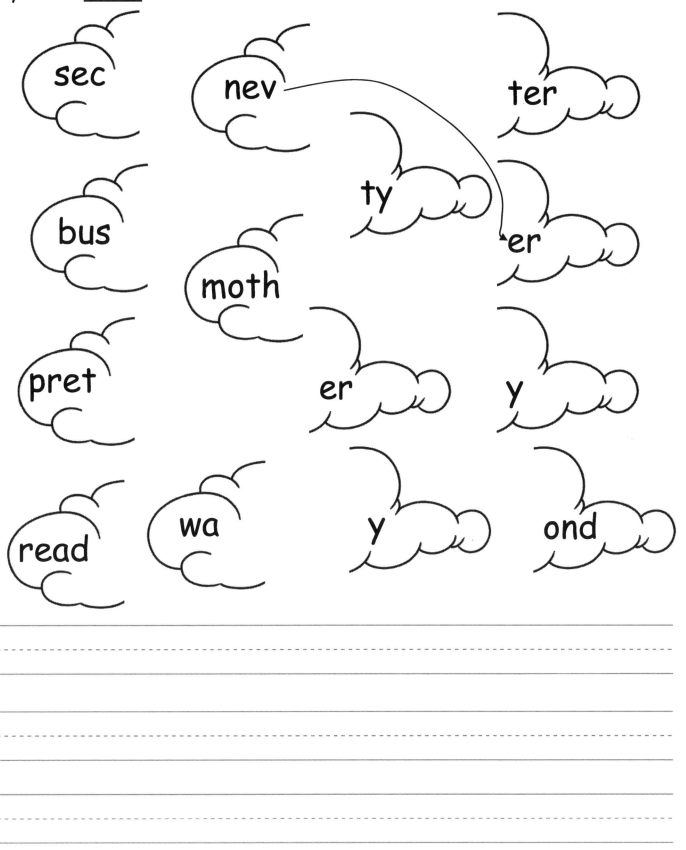

Say the word. Trace the word. Write the word.

yes yes

you you

Read the words. Look and think about how they are related. Find the word that does not belong and circle it.

pilot

a) police officer   b) teacher   c) man

duck

a) chicken   b) turkey   c) horse

milk

a) cheese   b) potatoes   c) butter

apple

a) rice   b) pear   c) orange

Read. Draw a line from the contraction to the two words for which it stands.

Contractions are shortened words , where you use an apostrophe (') in place of the missing letters.

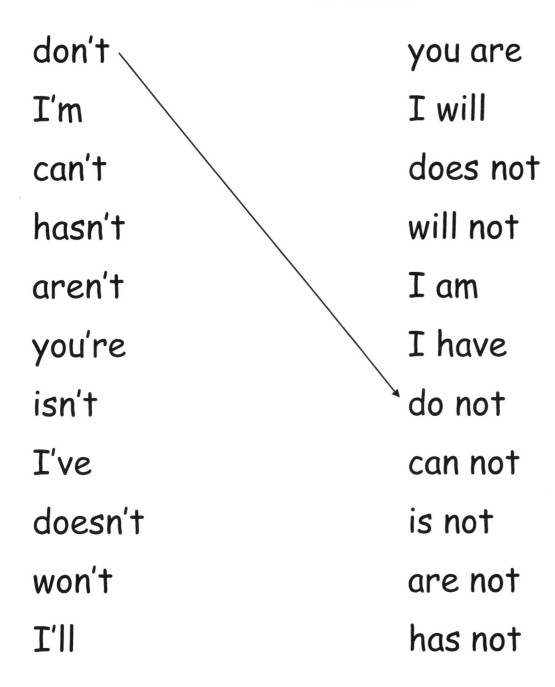

don't	you are
I'm	I will
can't	does not
hasn't	will not
aren't	I am
you're	I have
isn't	do not
I've	can not
doesn't	is not
won't	are not
I'll	has not

Say the number. Trace the number. Write the number.

I see 11 pineapples.

11 11 11 11 eleven eleven

Use pennies to measure each troll. Color the tallest troll.

___ pennies

__ pennies

Use pennies to find the price of each toy. Color the cheapest toy.

__ pennies

___ pennies

Count the items. Write the number word in the puzzle. Use the Choice Box to help you.

nine	five	eleven	six
three	eight	ten	seven

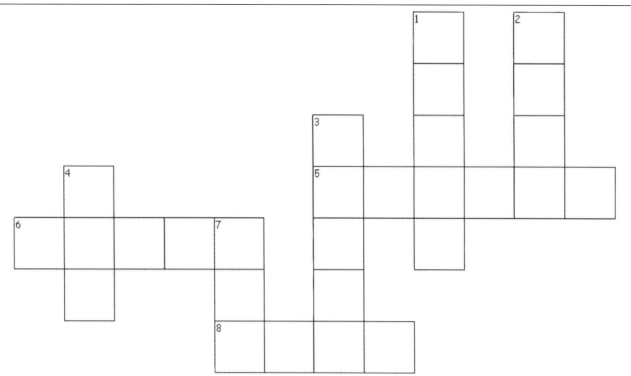

Down

1. ☀☀☀

2. 🪂🪂🪂🪂🪂

3. 🎫🎫🎫🎫🎫🎫🎫

4. ♡♡♡♡♡♡

7. ʃʃʃʃʃʃʃʃʃ

Across

5.

6.

8.

Color 1 snail brown.

How many snails are NOT colored?

Circle your answer.   1   2   3   4   5   6   7   8   9   10

How many snails are there in all?

Circle your answer.   10 11 12 13 14 15 16 17 18 19

Color 10 flowers red.

How many flowers are NOT colored?

Circle your answer.   1   2   3   4   5   6   7   8   9

How many flowers are there in all?

Circle your answer.   10 11 12 13 14 15 16 17 18 19

2 plus what number equals 3?

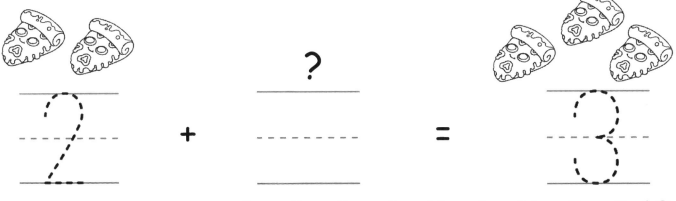

Circle your answer.   1   2   3   4   5   6   7   8   9 10

Count the objects. Write the number. Add and subtract the objects.

_____   _____   _____

- - - - - - - - - - -   +   - - - - - - - - - -   =   - - - - - - - - - -

_____   _____   _____

_____   _____   _____

- - - - - - - - - - -   -   - - - - - - - - - -   =   - - - - - - - - - -

_____   _____   _____

1 plus what number equals 4?

          ?

_____   _____   _____

1   +   - - - - - - - -   =   1

_____   _____   _____

Circle your answer.   0   1   2   3   4   5

Say the word. Trace the word. Write the word. Trace the shapes.

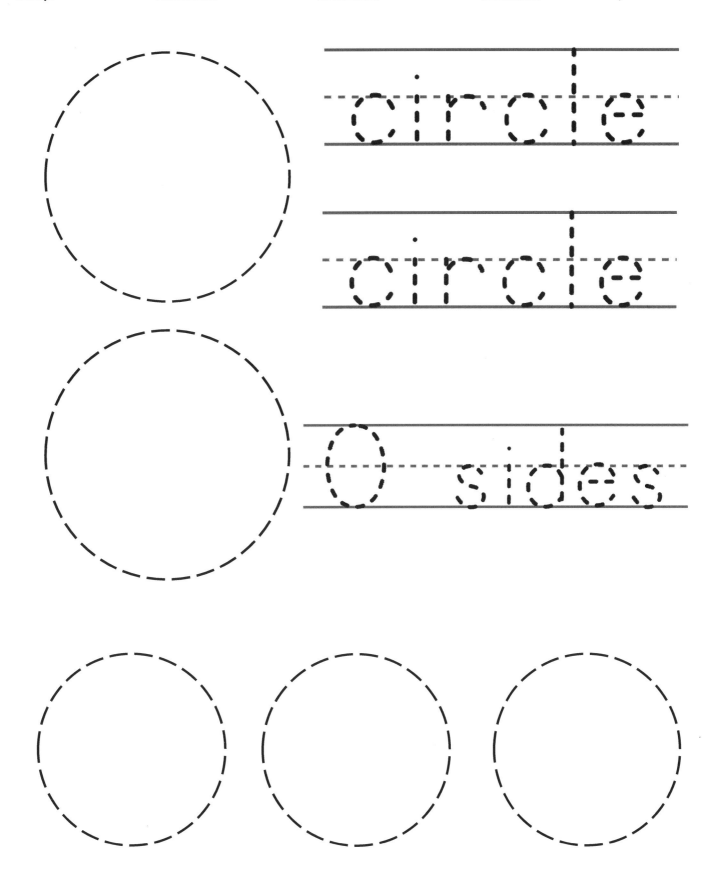

circle

circle

0 sides

Say the number. Trace the number. Write the number.

I see 12 cars.

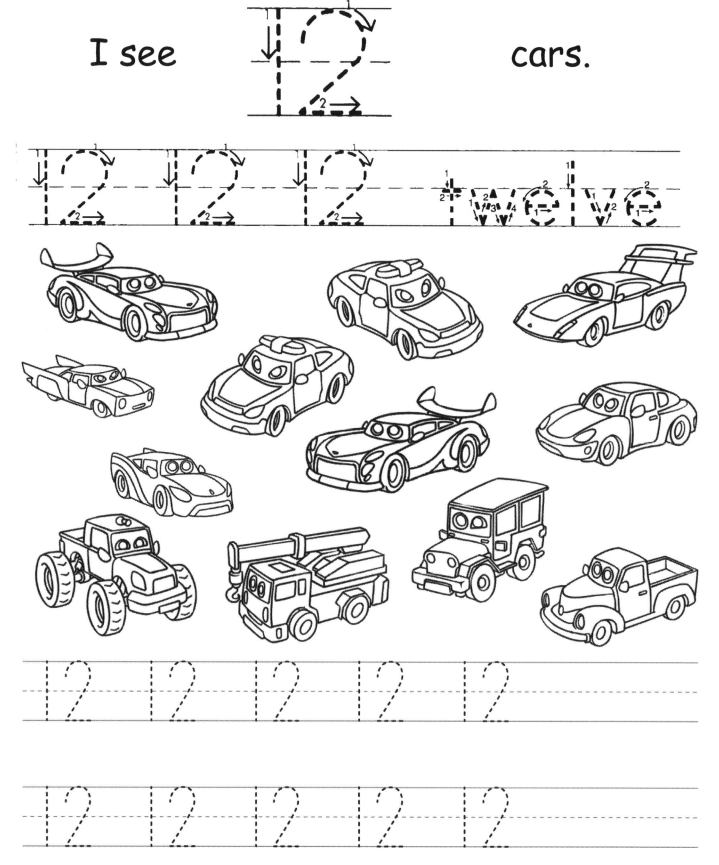

Say the word. Trace the word. Write the word. Trace the shapes.

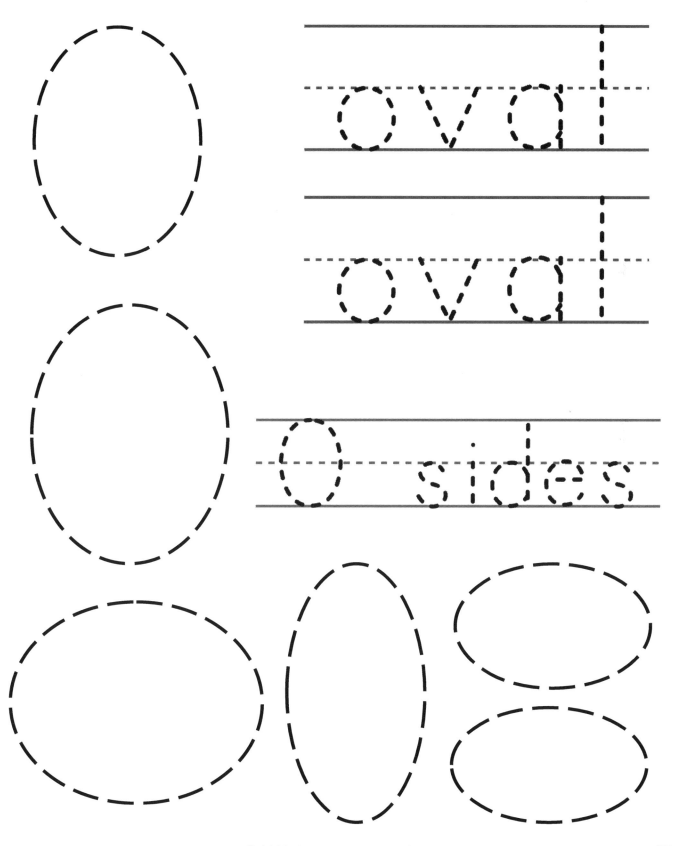

oval

oval

0 sides

Color 10 bananas yellow.

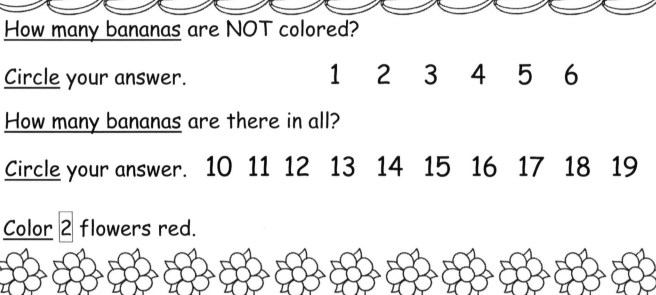

How many bananas are NOT colored?

Circle your answer.   1   2   3   4   5   6

How many bananas are there in all?

Circle your answer. 10 11 12 13 14 15 16 17 18 19

Color 2 flowers red.

How many flowers are NOT colored?

Circle your answer. 1   2   3   4   5   6   7   8   9   10

How many flowers are there in all?

Circle your answer. 10 11 12 13 14 15 16 17 18 19

3 plus what number equals 6?

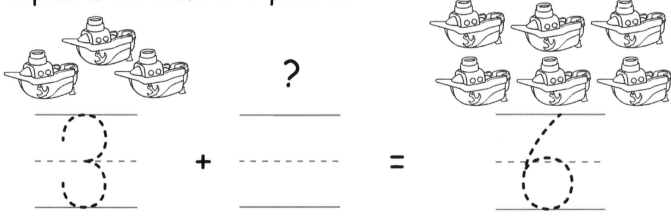

3 + ___ = 6

Circle your answer.   1   2   3   4   5   6   7   8   9 10

Count the objects. Write the number. Add and subtract the objects.

_____   +   _____   =   _____

- - - - - - -   - - - - - - -   - - - - - - -

_____   _____   _____

_____   -   _____   =   _____

- - - - - - -   - - - - - - -   - - - - - - -

_____   _____   _____

5 plus what number equals 7?

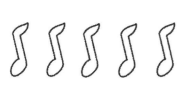   ?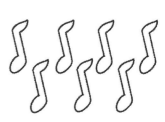

_____   +   _____   =   _____

Circle your answer.   0   1   2   3   4   5

Say the number. Trace the number. Write the number.

I see **13** trolls.

13 13 13 thirteen

13 13 13 13 13

13 13 13 13 13

Say the word. Trace the word. Write the word. Trace the shapes.

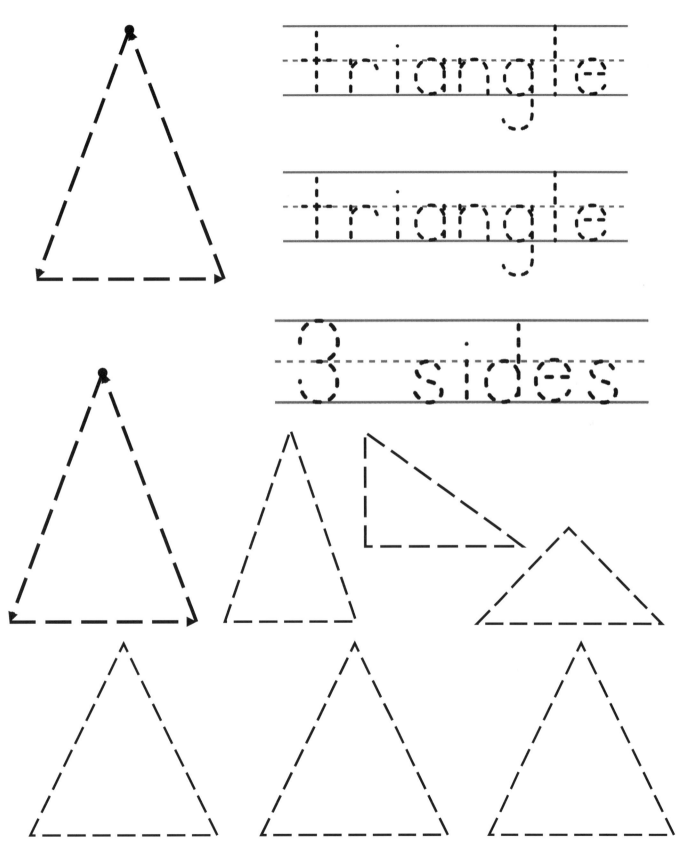

triangle

triangle

3 sides

My friends have a ton of stuffed toys. <u>Make</u> a chart of all our stuffed toys below. Liam's chart is done for you.

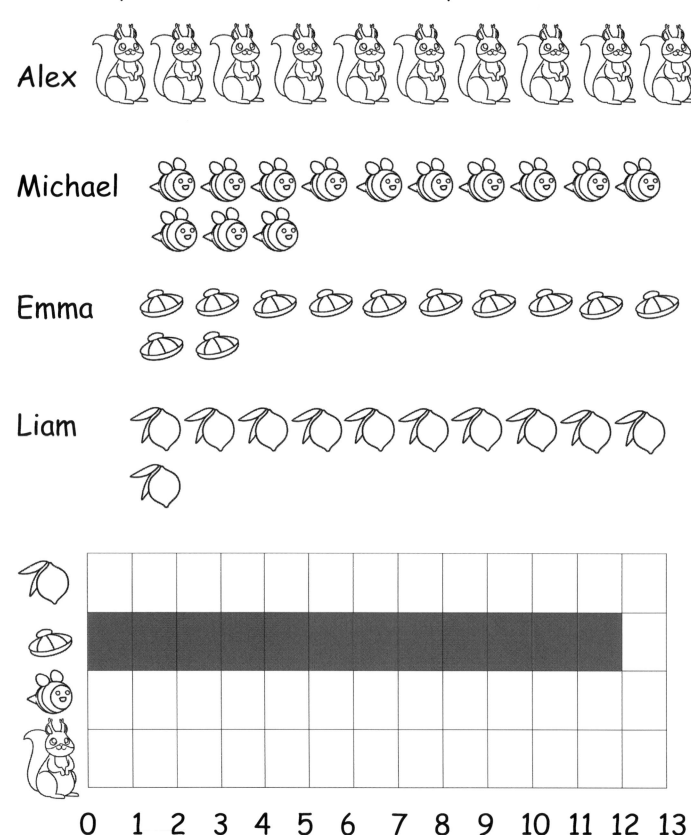

Alex

Michael

Emma

Liam

0 1 2 3 4 5 6 7 8 9 10 11 12 13

Color 10 flowers blue.

How many flowers are NOT colored?

Circle your answer.   2   3   4   5   6   7   8

How many flowers are there in all?

Circle your answer.   10 11 12 13 14 15 16 17 18 19

Color 3 bottles purple.

How many bottles are NOT colored?

Circle your answer.   1   2   3   4   5   6   7   8   9   10

How many bottles are there in all?

Circle your answer.   10 11 12 13 14 15 16 17 18 19

4 plus what number equals 6?

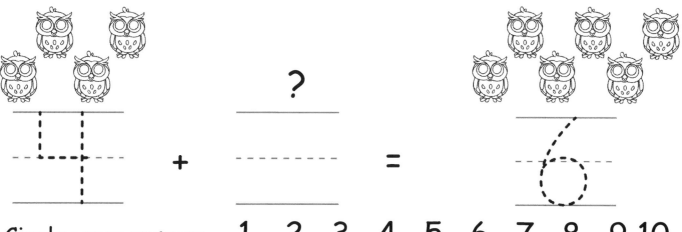

Circle your answer.   1   2   3   4   5   6   7   8   9 10

Count the objects. Write the number. Add and subtract the objects.

_____ + _____ = _____

- - - - - - - - -   - - - - - - - - -   - - - - - - - - -

_____   _____   _____

_____ - _____ = _____

- - - - - - - - -   - - - - - - - - -   - - - - - - - - -

_____   _____   _____

5 plus what number equals 8?

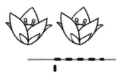

5 + _____ =

?

Circle your answer.   0   1   2   3   4   5

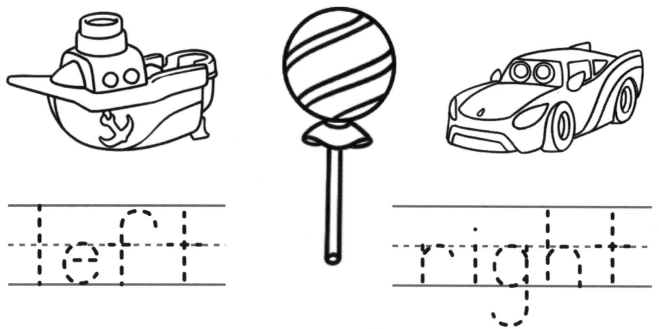

left

right

The boat is on the **LEFT** side of the candy.

The car is on the **RIGHT** side of the candy.

Color the **owl** on the **left** side of the circle.

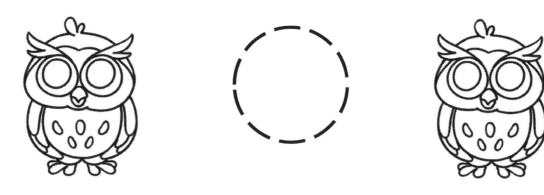

Color the **troll** on the **right** side of the triangle.

Say the number. Trace the number. Write the number.

I see 14 butterflies.

14   14   fourteen

My Grandma baked 2 apple pies. I ate a half of the pies. How many pies are left?

Circle your answer:

0   1   2   3   4   5

I found 6 shells. My brother broke a half of the shells. How many shells are left?

Circle your answer:

0   1   2   3   4   5

I got 4 cupcakes. I ate a half of them. How many cupcakes are left?

Circle your answer:

0   1   2   3   4   5

My birthday cake weighed 8 pounds! My friends ate a half of the cake. How many pounds are left?

Circle your answer: 0   1   2   3   4   5

Color 10 flowers red.

How many flowers are NOT colored?

Circle your answer.   2   3   4   5   6   7   8

How many flowers are there in all?

Circle your answer.   10 11 12 13 14 15 16 17 18 19

Color 4 cupcakes brown.

How many cupcakes are NOT colored?

Circle your answer.   1   2   3   4   5   6   7   8   9   10

How many cupcakes are there in all?

Circle your answer.   10 11 12 13 14 15 16 17 18 19

2 plus what number equals 7?

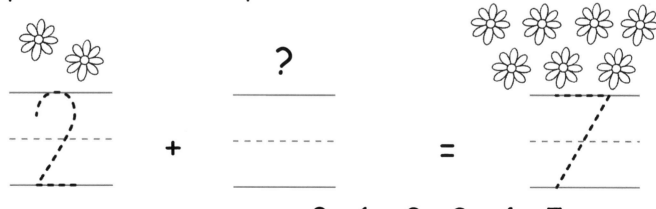

2   +   ?   =   7

Circle your answer.   0   1   2   3   4   5

Say the word. Trace the word. Write the word. Trace the shapes.

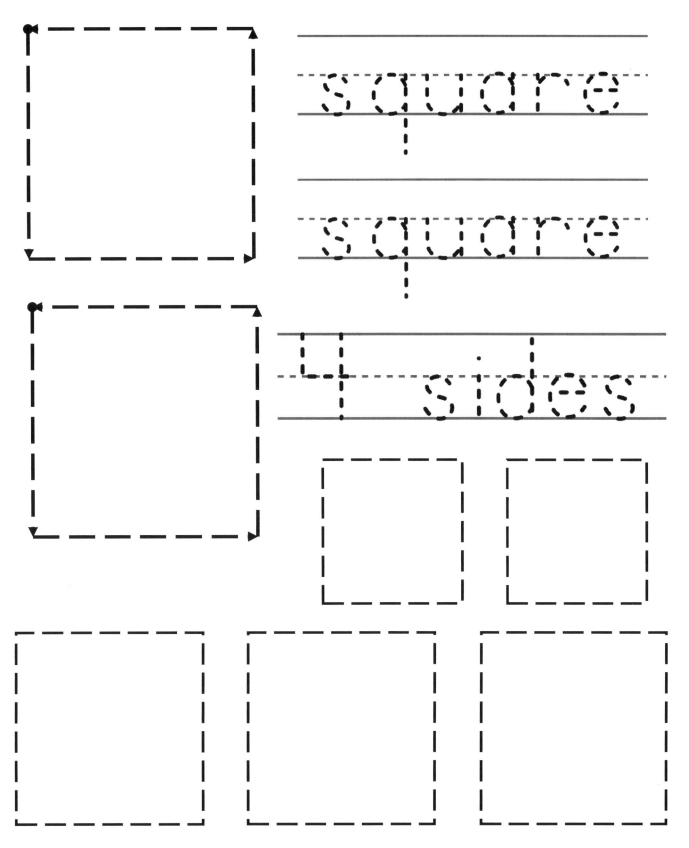

square

square

4 sides

Count the objects. Write the number. Add and subtract the objects.

_____   _____   _____

- - - - -   **+**   - - - - -   **=**   - - - - -

_____   _____   _____

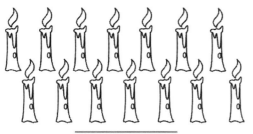   

- - - - -   **-**   - - - - -   **=**   - - - - -

_____   _____   _____

4 plus what number equals 8?

   **?**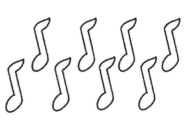

- -$\cdot 4\cdot$- -   **+**   - - - - -   **=**   - -8- -

_____   _____   _____

<u>Circle</u> your answer.   0   1   2   3   4   5

Say the word. Trace the word. Write the word. Trace the shapes.

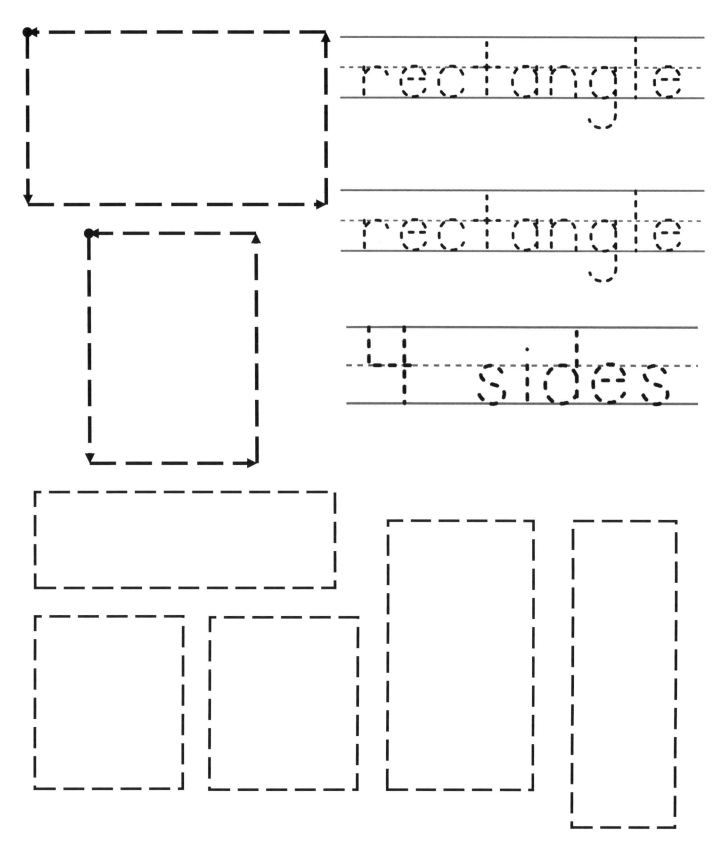

rectangle

rectangle

4 sides

Say the number. Trace the number. Write the number.

I see   15   fruits.

15 15 15 15 fifteen

15 15 15 15 15

15 15 15 15 15

© 2020 Home Run Press, LLC

Compare the items. <u>Write</u> the sign (>, <, or =) in the circle. <u>Use</u> > (greater than), < (less than), or = (equal to).

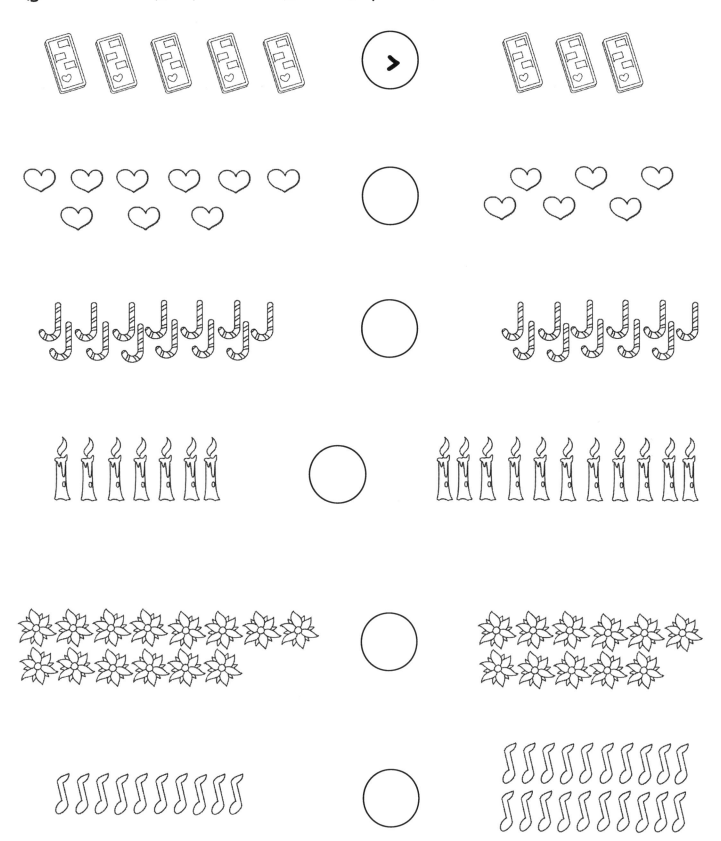

Color 5 lemons yellow.

How many lemons are NOT colored?

Circle your answer.   1 2   3   4   5   6   7   8   9   10

How many lemons are there in all?

Circle your answer.   10 11 12 13 14 15 16 17 18 19

Color 10 candies blue.

How many candies are NOT colored?

Circle your answer.   1 2   3   4   5   6   7   8   9   10

How many candies are there in all?

Circle your answer.   10 11 12 13 14 15 16 17 18 19

4 plus what number equals 9?

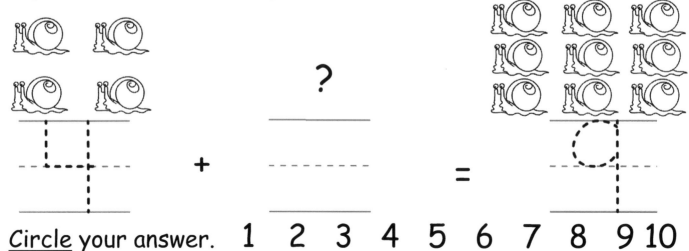

Circle your answer.   1   2   3   4   5   6   7   8   9 10

Count the objects. Write the number. Add and subtract the objects.

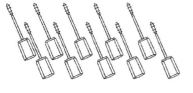

_____   _____   _____

__ __ __ __ __   +   __ __ __ __ __   =   __ __ __ __

_____   _____   _____

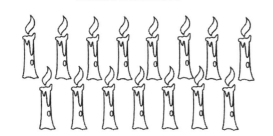

__ __ __ __ __   -   __ __ __ __ __   =   __ __ __ __

_____   _____   _____

6 plus what number equals 9?

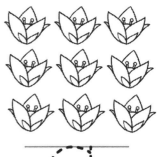

6   +   _____   =   9

<u>Circle</u> your answer.   0   1   2   3   4   5

Use nickels to measure each toy. Color the tallest toy.

__ nickels   __ nickels

Use nickels to find the price of each toy. Color the cheapest toy.

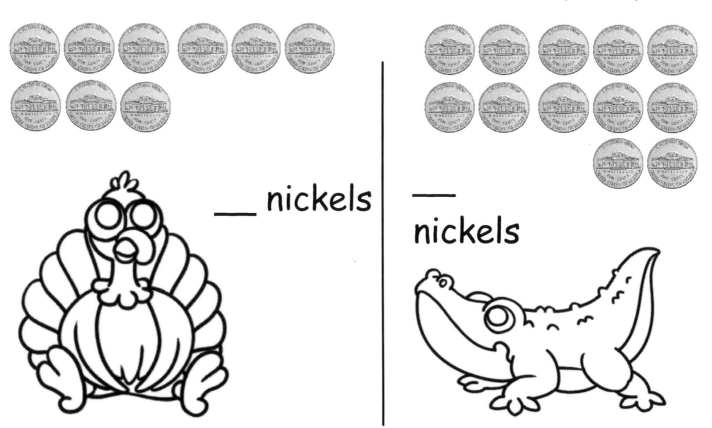

__ nickels   —
                  nickels

© 2020 Home Run Press, LLC

Say the number. Trace the number. Write the number.

I see **16** cherries.

16 16 16 sixteen

16 16 16 16 16

16 16 16 16 16

Color 6 strawberries red.

How many strawberries are NOT colored?

Circle your answer.   1 2   3   4   5   6   7   8   9   10

How many strawberries are there in all?

Circle your answer.   10 11 12 13 14 15 16 17 18 19

Color 10 candies green.

How many candies are NOT colored?

Circle your answer.   1 2   3   4   5   6   7   8   9   10

How many candies are there in all?

Circle your answer.   10 11 12 13 14 15 16 17 18 19

5 plus what number equals 7?

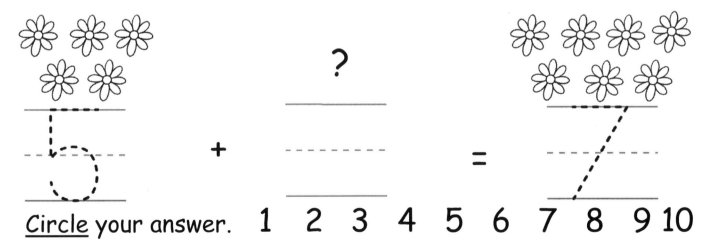

Circle your answer.   1   2   3   4   5   6   7   8   9 10

I am a number that is smaller than 5 and bigger than 3. What number am I?

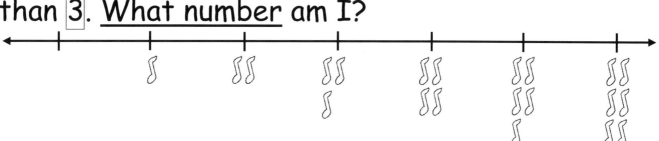

Circle your answer.   0 1 2 3 4 5 6 7

I am a number that is smaller than 11 and bigger than 9. What number am I?

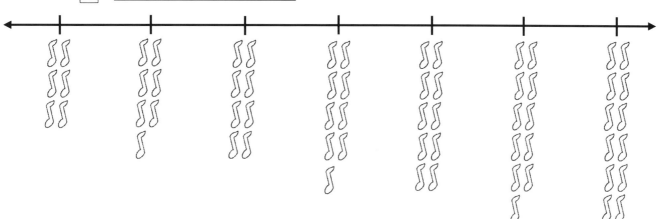

Circle your answer.   6 7 8 9 10 11 12 13

I am a number that is smaller than 15 and bigger than 13. What number am I?

Circle your answer.   9 10 11 12 13 14 15 16

Say the word. Trace the word. Write the word. Trace the shapes.

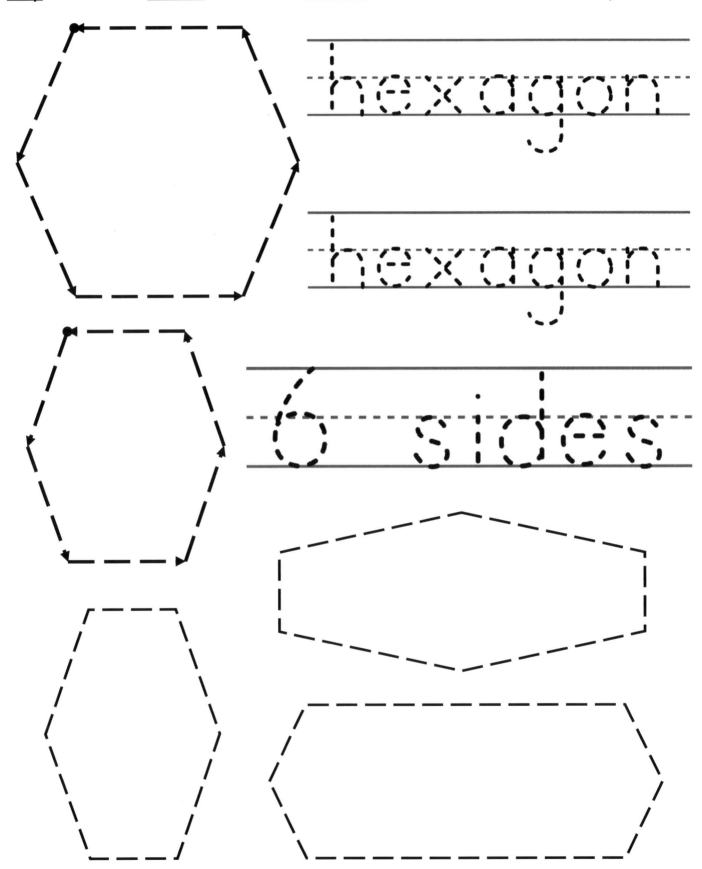

hexagon

hexagon

6 sides

Count the objects. Write the number. Add and subtract the objects.

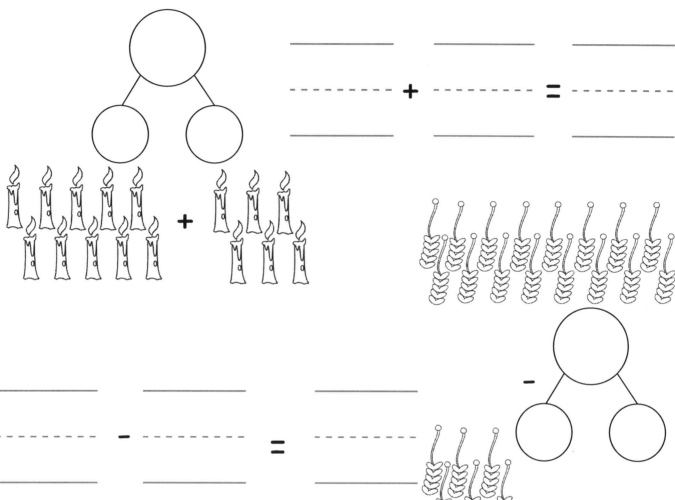

1 plus what number equals 8?

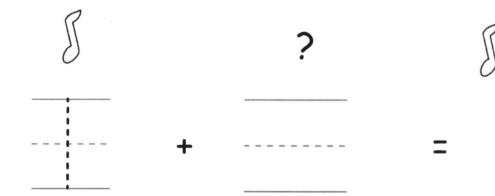

Circle your answer. 0 1 2 3 4 5 6 7 8

Say the number. Trace the number. Write the number.

I see 17 cupcakes.

17 17 seventeen

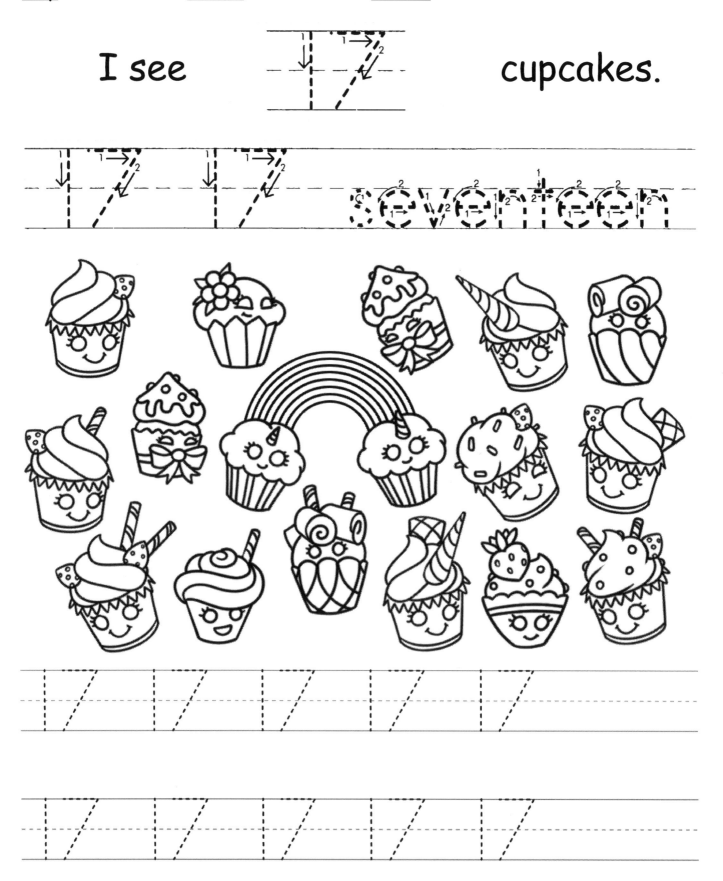

© 2020 Home Run Press, LLC

How many butterflies are there?

Circle your answer.   5   6   7   8   9   10   11   12

Color each heart red. How many hearts are there?

Circle your answer.   8   9   10   11   12   13   14   15

Color each bigger wing yellow. How many bigger wings are there?

Circle your answer.   8   9   10   11   12   13   14   15

2 plus what number equals 8?

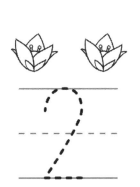   +   
   =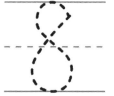

Circle your answer.   1   2   3   4   5   6   7   8   9   10

Use dimes to measure each troll. Color the shortest troll.

__ dimes

__ dimes

Use dimes to find the price of each toy. Color the cheapest toy.

__ dimes

__ dimes

Color 7 cherries red.

How many cherries are NOT colored?

Circle your answer.　1　2　3　4　5　6　7　8　9　10

How many cherries are there in all?

Circle your answer.　10　11　12　13　14　15　16　17　18　19

Color 10 flowers yellow.

How many flowers are NOT colored?

Circle your answer.　1　2　3　4　5　6　7　8　9　10

How many flowers are there in all?

Circle your answer.　10　11　12　13　14　15　16　17　18　19

10 plus what number equals 14?

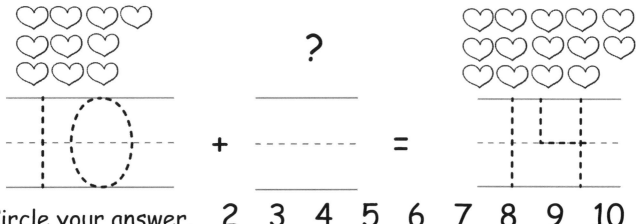

Circle your answer.　2　3　4　5　6　7　8　9　10

Count the objects. Write the number. Add and subtract the objects.

-------- + -------- = --------

-------- - -------- = --------

4 plus what number equals 9?

4 + _____ = 9

Circle your answer.   0   1   2   3   4   5   6   7

Say the number. Trace the number. Write the number.

I see   18   flowers.

18   18   18   eighteen

18 18 18 18 18

18 18 18 18 18

I am a number that is smaller than 8 and bigger than 6.
__What number__ am I?

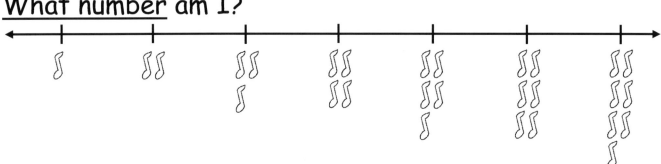

__Circle__ your answer.   0   1   2   3   4   5   6   7

I am a number that is smaller than 15 and bigger than
13. __What number__ am I?

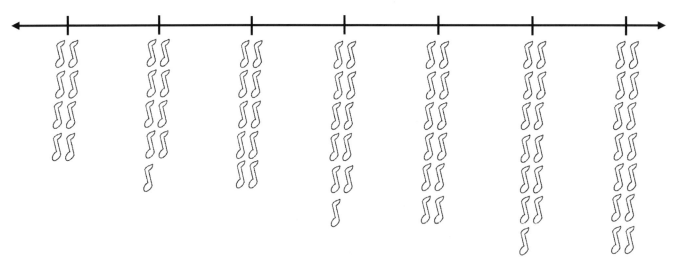

__Circle__ your answer.   8   9   10 11 12 13 14 15

I am a number that is smaller than 18 and bigger than
16. __What number__ am I?

__Circle__ your answer.   12 13 14 15 16 17 18 19

Color 8 cherries.

How many cherries are NOT colored?

Circle your answer.   1 2   3   4   5   6   7   8   9   10

How many cherries are there in all?

Circle your answer.   10 11 12 13 14 15 16 17 18 19

Color 10 candies.

How many candies are NOT colored?

Circle your answer.   1 2   3   4   5   6   7   8   9   10

How many candies are there in all?

Circle your answer.   10 11 12 13 14 15 16 17 18 19

3 plus what number equals 7?

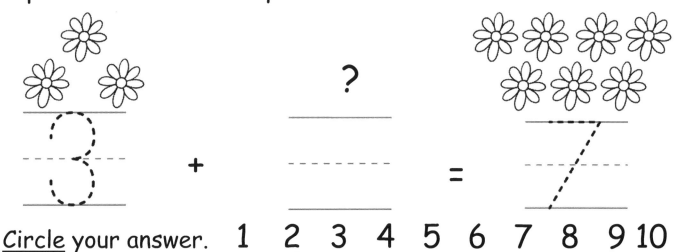

Circle your answer.   1   2   3   4   5   6   7   8   9 10

Count the objects. Write the number. Add and subtract the objects.

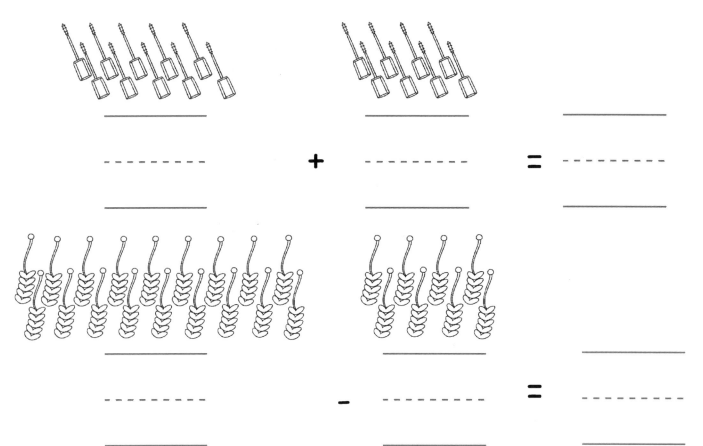

_____ + _____ = _____

_____ - _____ = _____

10 plus what number equals 12?

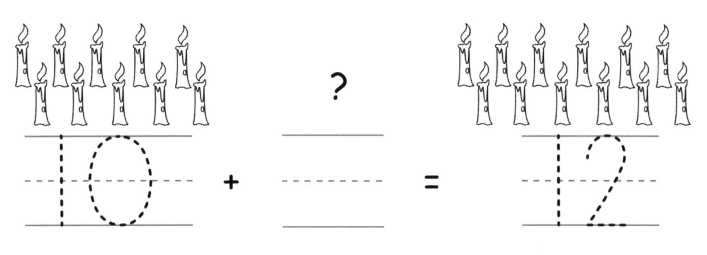

Circle your answer. 1 2 3 4 5 6 7 8 9 10

Say the number. Trace the number. Write the number.

I see   19   crayons.

19   19   nineteen

19   19   19   19   19

19   19   19   19   19

Color each star yellow. <u>How many stars</u> are there?

Circle your answer. 5 6 7 8 9 10 11 12

Color each Christmas tree ball red. <u>How many balls</u> are there?

Circle your answer. 8 9 10 11 12 13 14 15

Color each cloud blue. <u>How many clouds</u> are there?

Circle your answer. 1 2 3 4 5 6 7 8

Color the cloud with the **greatest** number in each row.

15   18   12

13   14   19

11   15   10

12   15   18

17   13   16

Color 9 candies green.

J J J J J J J J J J J J J J J J J J J

How many candies are NOT colored?

Circle your answer.   1 2   3   4   5   6   7   8   9   10

How many candies are there in all?

Circle your answer.   11 12 13 14 15 16 17 18 19

Color 10 cherries red.

How many cherries are NOT colored?

Circle your answer.   1 2   3   4   5   6   7   8   9   10

How many cherries are there in all?

Circle your answer.   11 12 13 14 15 16 17 18 19

10 plus what number equals 18?

?

10 + ____ = 18

Circle your answer.   1   2   3   4   5   6   7   8   9 10

Count the objects. Write the number. Add and subtract the objects.

_____   _____   _____

- - - - - - -   +   - - - - - - -   =   - - - - - - -

_____   _____   _____

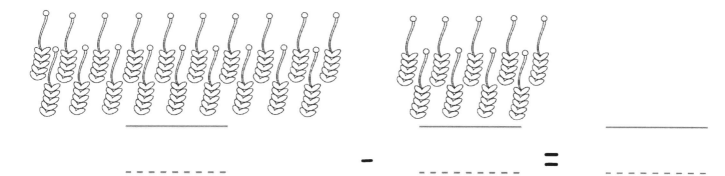

- - - - - - -   -   - - - - - - -   =   - - - - - - -

_____   _____   _____

10 plus what number equals 13?

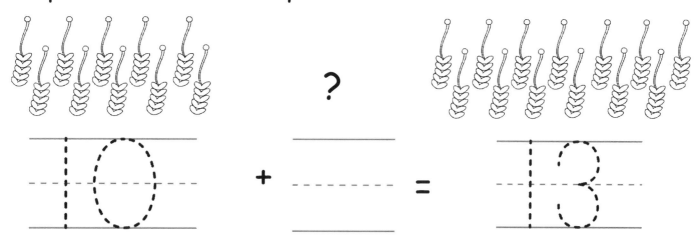

10   +   _____   =   13

Circle your answer.   1   2   3   4   5   6   7   8   9 10

Say the number. Trace the number. Write the number.

I see **20** candies.

20 20 twenty

20 20 20 20

20 20 20 20

Color 10 cherries.

How many cherries are NOT colored?

Circle your answer.   1 2   3   4   5   6   7   8   9   10

How many cherries are there in all?

Circle your answer.   12 13 14 15 16 17 18 19 20

Color 10 candies.

How many candies are NOT colored?

Circle your answer.   1 2   3   4   5   6   7   8   9   10

How many candies are there in all?

Circle your answer.   12 13 14 15 16 17 18 19 20

10 plus what number equals 11?

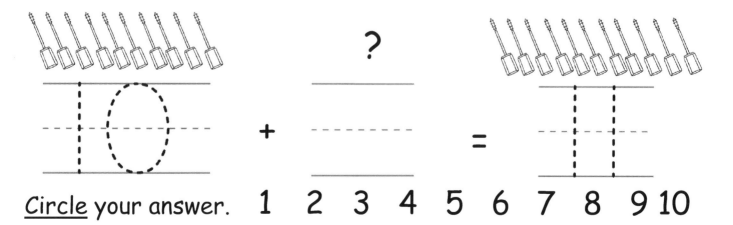

Circle your answer.   1   2   3   4   5   6   7   8   9 10

Color the cloud with the **least** number in each row.

15   16   12

13   14   10

11   15   19

12   15   10

17   13   18

10 plus what number equals 15?

 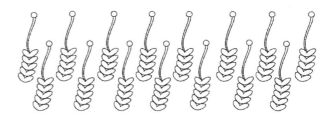

10 + ____ = 15

Circle your answer.   2   3   4   5   6   7   8   9   10

10 plus what number equals 17?

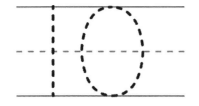 ?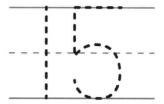

10 + ____ = 17

Circle your answer.   2   3   4   5   6   7   8   9   10

How many legs do the 3 squirrels have altogether?

Circle your answer.   7   8   9   10   11   12   13   14   15

Count the objects. Write the number. Add and subtract the objects.

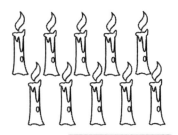

‾‾‾‾‾‾‾‾‾

- - - - - - -   +   - - - - - - -   =   - - - - - - -

‾‾‾‾‾‾‾‾‾   ‾‾‾‾‾‾‾‾‾

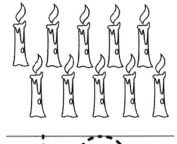

‾‾‾‾‾‾‾‾‾   ‾‾‾‾‾‾‾‾‾

- - - - - - -   -   - - - - - - -   =   - - - - - - -

‾‾‾‾‾‾‾‾‾   ‾‾‾‾‾‾‾‾‾

10 plus what number equals 16?

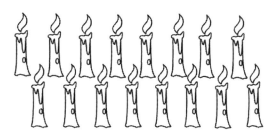

?

10   +   - - - - -   =   16

Circle your answer.   1   2   3   4   5   6   7   8   9 10

10 plus what number equals 19?

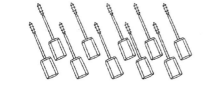 ?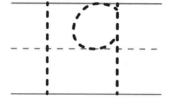

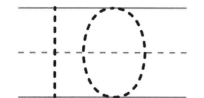

10 + ____ = 19

Circle your answer.   1   2   3   4   5   6   7   8   9   10

10 plus what number equals 20?

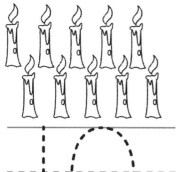 

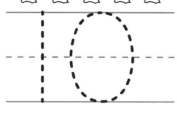

10 + ____ = 20

Circle your answer.   1   2   3   4   5   6   7   8   9 10

How many groups of 5 can be made out of 10 cupcakes?

Circle your answer.   1   2   3   4   5   6   7   8

Say the word. Trace the word. Write the word.

am am

are are

and and

ask ask

Read each sentence. Write the missing word ("am" or "are").

Racoons are always hungry.

I am happy to see you.

Some of the words have **ask** hidden inside. Find the words and underline **ask** in them.

t<u>ask</u>   b<u>ask</u>et   m<u>ask</u>

Al<u>ask</u>a   master   masque   land

29

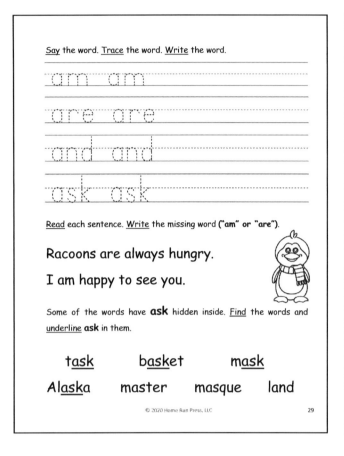

Say the word. Trace the word. Write the word.

black black

brown brown

Read each sentence. Write the missing word ("black" or "brown").

Pandas are black and white bears.

Most monkeys are brown.

Here are some words that start with letter **C**. Say them aloud. Then trace each word.

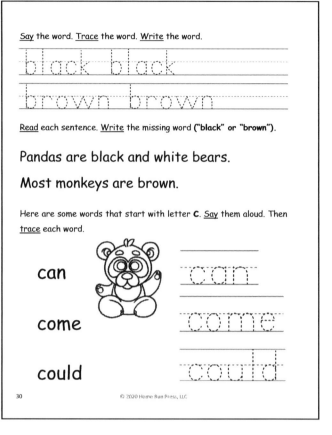

can   can

come   come

could   could

30

Say the word. Trace the word. Write the word.

be be

but but

Read the words. Look and think about how they are related. Find the word that does not belong and circle it.

carrot

a) peach   b) cabbage   c) onion

fish

a) frog   b) snake   c) zebra

doctor

a) artist   b) mail   c) farmer

truck

a) ship   b) bus   c) car

31

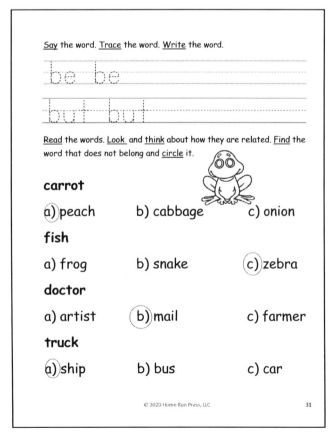

Say the word. Trace the word. Write the word.

day day

eat eat

first first

Read each sentence. Write the missing word ("day" or "eat").

Lions like to spend the day under a tree.

When the sun goes down, they eat.

Read each sentence. Write the missing word ("first").

One is the first number.

This is my first cupcake.

When I eat, I first wash my hands.

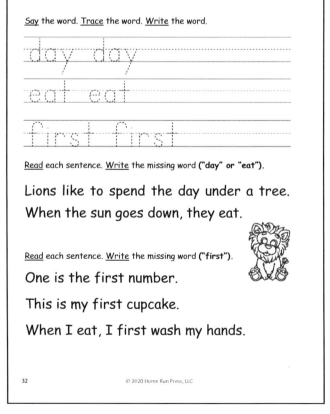

32

get get

give give

go go

good good

Find each word in the word search.

ARE   CAN   COME   DAY   BLACK

BROWN   FIRST   GET   GOOD

```
Q  Q  W  X  Z  Y  G  X  F  X  O  J
V  C  F  G  Y  S  U  I  P  F  Q  E
X  X  S  N  W  O  R  B  D  O  G  C
P  E  U  W  A  S  C  L  A  R  E  C
V  T  E  C  T  C  L  D  Y  M  T  M
Z  P  U  O  W  A  D  O  O  G  K  F
R  L  Z  F  X  N  K  C  A  L  B  O
```

---

have have

help help

Draw a line to connect opposite words.

Antonyms are words that have opposite meanings.

new   throw

easy   boring

clean   sick

bright   rainy

sunny   dark

catch   old

funny   hard

well   dirty

Add each beginning letter or letters to the word ending to write new words.

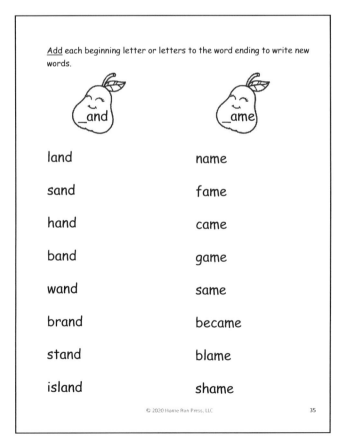

_and   _ame

land   name

sand   fame

hand   came

band   game

wand   same

brand   became

stand   blame

island   shame

---

like like

look look

Draw a line to connect words that are the **same or synonyms**. Say the words.

Synonyms are words that mean exactly or almost the same.

van   draw

learn   leave

color   sneakers

make   jog

run   build

shoes   truck

go   study

Say the word. Trace the word. Write the word.

make make

must must

Draw a line to connect words that **rhyme**. Say the words.

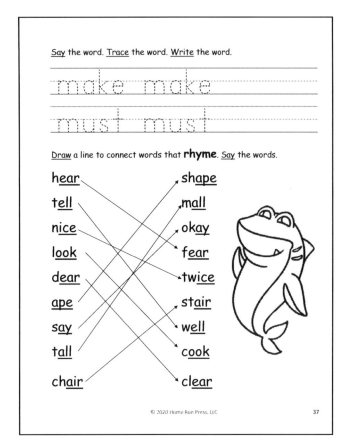

hear   shape
tell   mall
nice   okay
look   fear
dear   twice
ape   stair
say   well
tall   cook
chair   clear

Say the word. Trace the word. Write the word.

name name

number number

2. Draw a line from the snail to the pear with the letters that finish the word.

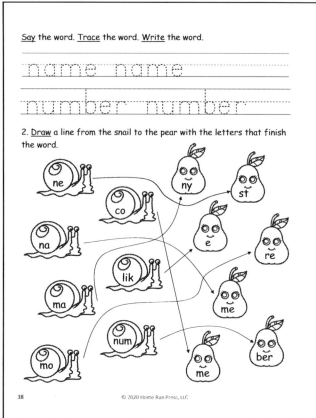

Add each beginning letter or letters to the word ending to write new words.

jar   air
far   fir
war   fair
near   hair
hear   chair
fear   pair
dear   their
wear   heir

Say the word. Trace the word. Write the word.

people people

please please

Read the words. Write the missing letters to write the word from the Choice Box.

old   play   out   must   help

part   have   people   please

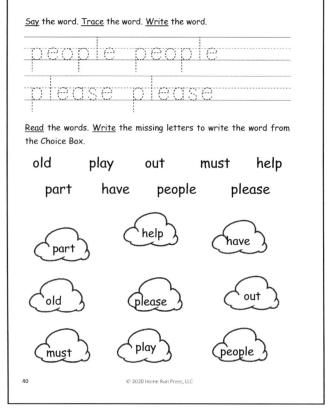

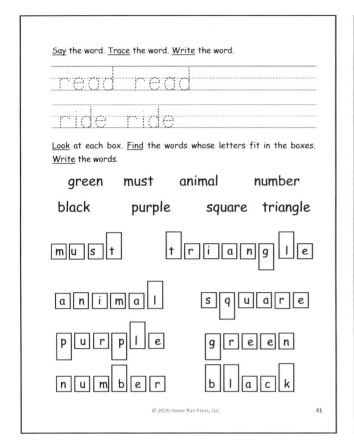

Say the word. Trace the word. Write the word.

read read

ride ride

Look at each box. Find the words whose letters fit in the boxes. Write the words.

| green | must | animal | number |

| black | purple | square | triangle |

m u s t   t r i a n g l e

a n i m a l   s q u a r e

p u r p l e   g r e e n

n u m b e r   b l a c k

41

Say the word. Trace the word. Write the word.

she she

some some

Use the words from the Choice Box to unscramble the words below.

| about | all | after | again | build |
| always | ask | blue | buy | before |

forebe   before   kas   ask

fater   after   lal   all

outba   about   belu   blue

salway   always   aagin   again

dilub   build   uby   buy

42

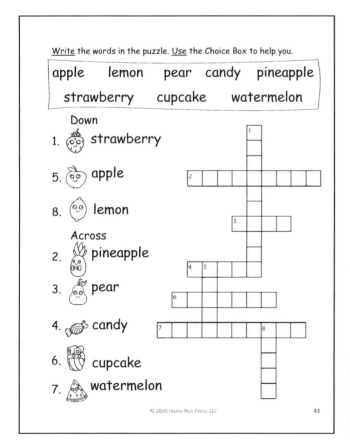

Write the words in the puzzle. Use the Choice Box to help you.

| apple | lemon | pear | candy | pineapple |
| strawberry | cupcake | watermelon | | |

Down
1. strawberry
5. apple
8. lemon

Across
2. pineapple
3. pear
4. candy
6. cupcake
7. watermelon

43

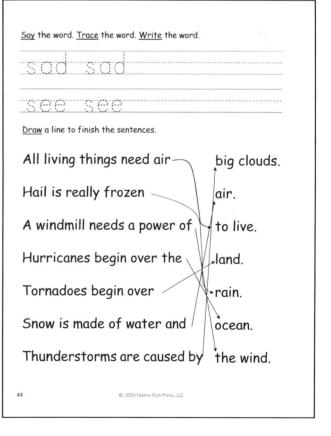

Say the word. Trace the word. Write the word.

sad sad

see see

Draw a line to finish the sentences.

All living things need air   big clouds.

Hail is really frozen   air.

A windmill needs a power of   to live.

Hurricanes begin over the   land.

Tornadoes begin over   rain.

Snow is made of water and   ocean.

Thunderstorms are caused by   the wind.

44

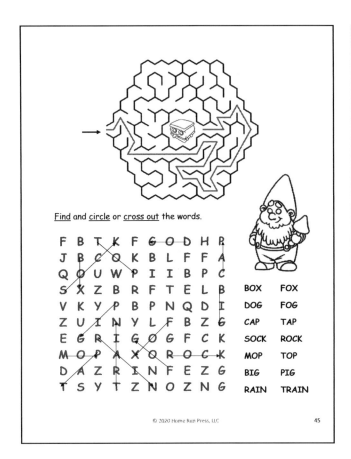

Find and circle or cross out the words.

```
F  B  T  K  F  G  O  D  H  R
J  B  C  O  K  B  L  F  F  A
Q  O  U  W  P  I  I  B  P  C
S  X  Z  B  R  F  T  E  L  B
V  K  Y  P  B  P  N  Q  D  I
Z  U  I  N  Y  L  F  B  Z  G
E  G  R  I  G  O  G  F  C  K
M  O  P  A  X  O  R  O  C  K
D  A  Z  R  I  N  F  E  Z  G
T  S  Y  T  Z  N  O  Z  N  G
```

BOX	FOX
DOG	FOG
CAP	TAP
SOCK	ROCK
MOP	TOP
BIG	PIG
RAIN	TRAIN

Say the word. Trace the word. Write the word.

they   they

two   two

Color the lemons with the word inside.

than – red	money – blue
time – green	tree – yellow
mail – pink	train - brown

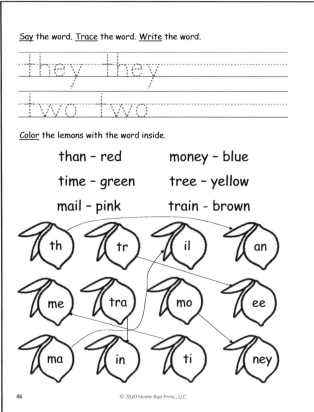

Say the word. Trace the word. Write the word.

these   these

this   this

Read the words. Look and think about how they are related. Find the word that does not belong and circle it.

large

a) big   b) small   c) huge

library

a) school   b) house   c) cafe

hospital

a) playground   b) post office   c) library

boat

a) ship   b) tanker   c) tractor

Say the word. Trace the word. Write the word.

than   than

Each word below is written in a secret code. Replace each letter in the words with the letter that comes **after** it in the alphabet. Write the words.

eqhdmc	friend
ehqrs	first
fqnv	grow
bghkc	child
bntkc	could
annj	book
lnqd	more

Say the word. Trace the word. Write the word.

use use

want want

A _verb_ is a word that _shows action_.

Circle the **verb or verbs** in each sentence.

Flowers (have) seeds inside them.

Dirt (is made) of very small pieces of rock.

Many kinds of animals (live) in forests.

Waves (form) at sea as winds (blow).

River water (comes) from rainwater.

Icebergs (are) large mountains of ice.

Mountains (are made) from rock.

© 2020 Home Run Press, LLC   49

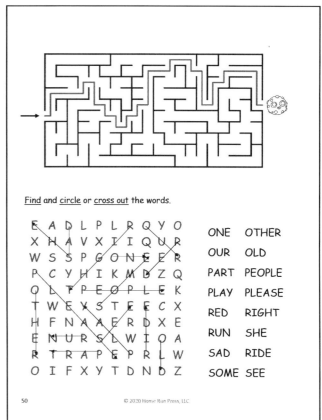

Find and circle or cross out the words.

E	A	D	L	P	L	R	Q	Y	O
X	H	A	V	X	I	I	Q	U	R
W	S	S	P	G	O	N	E	E	R
P	C	Y	H	I	K	M	B	Z	Q
O	L	T	P	E	O	P	L	E	K
T	W	E	X	S	T	E	E	C	X
H	F	N	A	A	E	R	D	X	E
E	N	U	R	S	L	W	I	O	A
R	T	R	A	P	E	P	R	L	W
O	I	F	X	Y	T	D	N	D	Z

ONE   OTHER
OUR   OLD
PART   PEOPLE
PLAY   PLEASE
RED   RIGHT
RUN   SHE
SAD   RIDE
SOME   SEE

50   © 2020 Home Run Press, LLC

Say the word. Trace the word. Write the word.

what what

when when

Unscramble and complete each sentence.

Rocks are made of minerals.
              emad

Minerals ____ have different shapes and
              heav
colors.
    crolos

Lava is melted ____ rock. It ____ comes out
              kocr   cemos
from the center of the ____ earth. Hot
                        earht
gases inside the ____ earth push the
                  tearh
lava out.
    vala

© 2020 Home Run Press, LLC   51

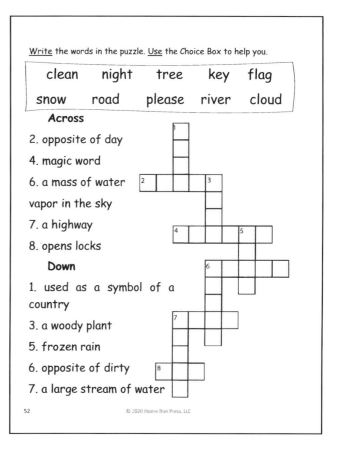

Write the words in the puzzle. Use the Choice Box to help you.

clean	night	tree	key	flag
snow	road	please	river	cloud

Across

2. opposite of day
4. magic word
6. a mass of water vapor in the sky
7. a highway
8. opens locks

Down

1. used as a symbol of a country
3. a woody plant
5. frozen rain
6. opposite of dirty
7. a large stream of water

52   © 2020 Home Run Press, LLC

115

which which

white white

2. Rewrite the words in **alphabetical order**.

forest	1. ant
ant	2. bee
brother	3. brother
bee	4. come
water	5. forest
saw	6. get
toy	7. saw
get	8. toy
come	9. water

© 2020 Home Run Press, LLC   53

---

well well

Each word below is written in a secret code. Replace each letter in the words with the letter that comes **before** it in the alphabet. Write the words.

qmfbtf	please
upebz	today
nvtu	must
esbx	draw
mpoh	long
mfgu	left
sjhiu	right

54   © 2020 Home Run Press, LLC

Draw a line to match the first syllable of each word to the second syllable. Write the words below.

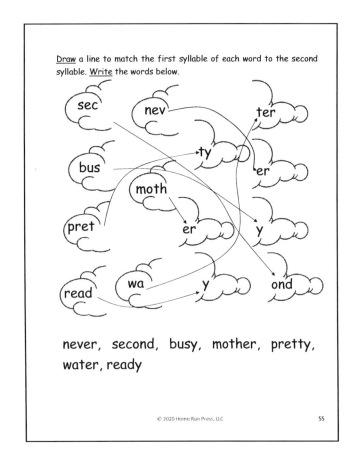

never, second, busy, mother, pretty, water, ready

© 2020 Home Run Press, LLC   55

---

yes yes

you you

Read the words. Look and think about how they are related. Find the word that does not belong and circle it.

pilot
a) police officer   b) teacher   c) man

duck
a) chicken   b) turkey   c) horse

milk
a) cheese   b) potatoes   c) butter

apple
a) rice   b) pear   c) orange

56   © 2020 Home Run Press, LLC

Read. Draw a line from the contraction to the two words for which it stands.

Contractions are shortened words , where you use an apostrophe (') in place of the missing letters.

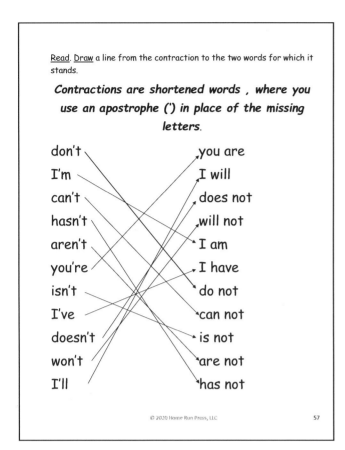

don't   you are
I'm   I will
can't   does not
hasn't   will not
aren't   I am
you're   I have
isn't   do not
I've   can not
doesn't   is not
won't   are not
I'll   has not

Say the number. Trace the number. Write the number.

I see ⬇️⬇️ 11 pineapples.

11 11 eleven eleven

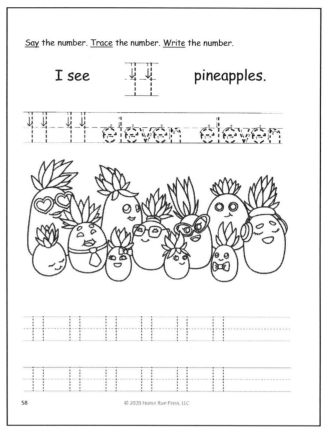

Use pennies to measure each troll. Color the tallest troll.

6 pennies   4 pennies

Use pennies to find the price of each toy. Color the cheapest toy.

11 pennies   10 pennies

Count the items. Write the number word in the puzzle. Use the Choice Box to help you.

nine	five	eleven	six
three	eight	ten	seven

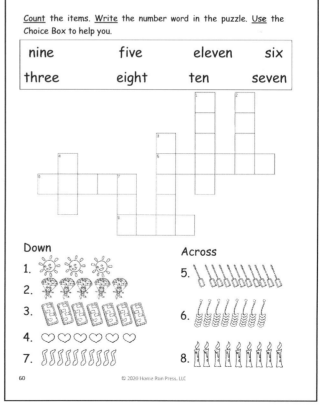

Down
1.
2.
3.
4.
7.

Across
5.
6.
8.

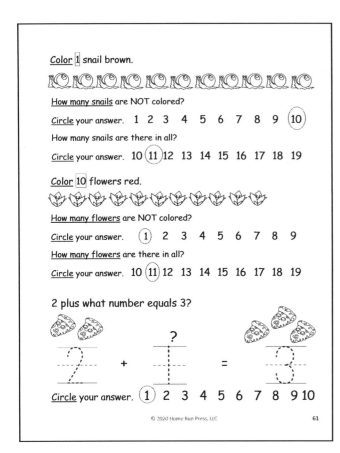

Color 1 snail brown.

How many snails are NOT colored?

Circle your answer. 1 2 3 4 5 6 7 8 9 (10)

How many snails are there in all?

Circle your answer. 10 (11) 12 13 14 15 16 17 18 19

Color 10 flowers red.

How many flowers are NOT colored?

Circle your answer. (1) 2 3 4 5 6 7 8 9

How many flowers are there in all?

Circle your answer. 10 (11) 12 13 14 15 16 17 18 19

2 plus what number equals 3?

2 + 1 = 3

Circle your answer. (1) 2 3 4 5 6 7 8 9 10

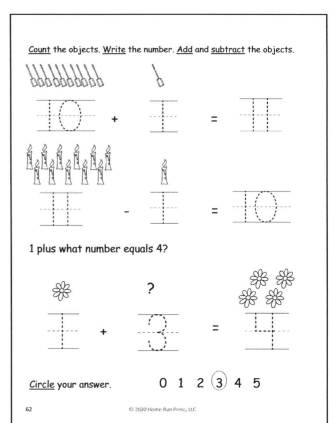

Count the objects. Write the number. Add and subtract the objects.

10 + 1 = 11

11 - 1 = 10

1 plus what number equals 4?

1 + 3 = 4

Circle your answer.   0 1 2 (3) 4 5

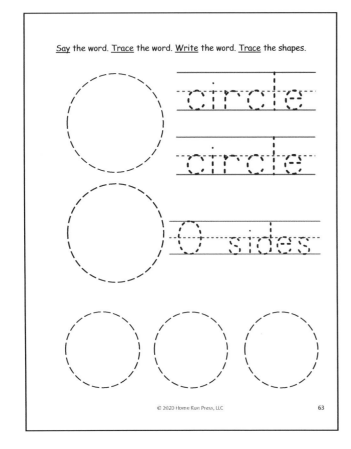

Say the word. Trace the word. Write the word. Trace the shapes.

circle

circle

0 sides

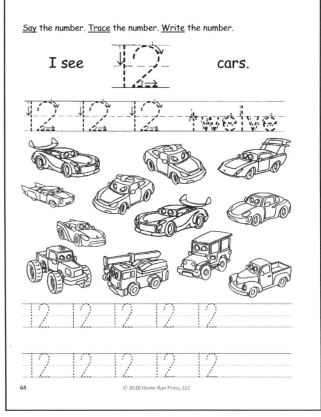

Say the number. Trace the number. Write the number.

I see 12 cars.

12 12 12 twelve

12 12 12 12 12

12 12 12 12 12

118

Say the word. Trace the word. Write the word. Trace the shapes.

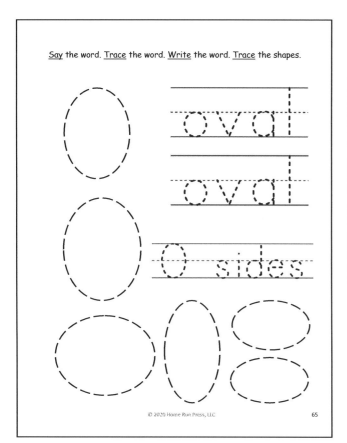

Color 10 bananas yellow.

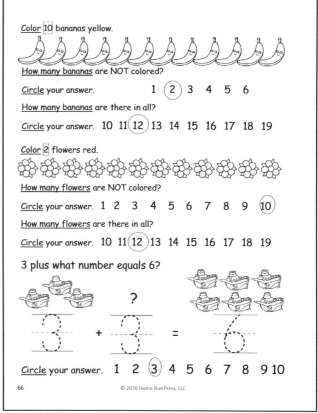

How many bananas are NOT colored?

Circle your answer. 1 (2) 3 4 5 6

How many bananas are there in all?

Circle your answer. 10 11 (12) 13 14 15 16 17 18 19

Color 2 flowers red.

How many flowers are NOT colored?

Circle your answer. 1 2 3 4 5 6 7 8 9 (10)

How many flowers are there in all?

Circle your answer. 10 11 (12) 13 14 15 16 17 18 19

3 plus what number equals 6?

$$3 + 3 = 6$$

Circle your answer. 1 2 (3) 4 5 6 7 8 9 10

Count the objects. Write the number. Add and subtract the objects.

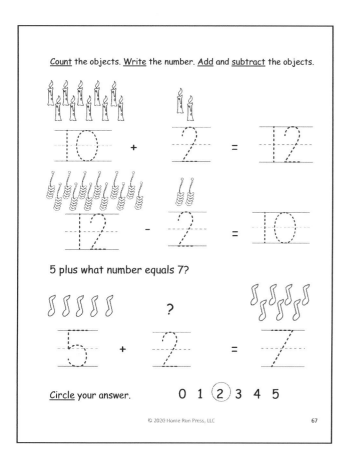

$$10 + 2 = 12$$

$$12 - 2 = 10$$

5 plus what number equals 7?

$$5 + 2 = 7$$

Circle your answer.   0 1 (2) 3 4 5

Say the number. Trace the number. Write the number.

I see 13 trolls.

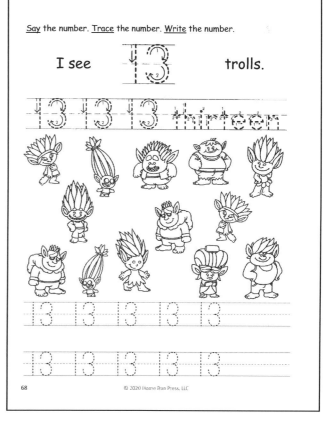

13 13 13 thirteen

13 13 13 13 13

13 13 13 13 13

© 2020 Home Run Press, LLC

Say the word. Trace the word. Write the word. Trace the shapes.

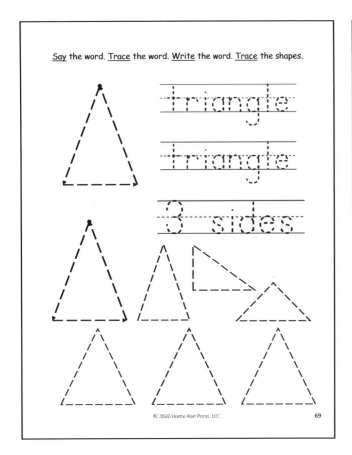

triangle

triangle

3 sides

My friends have a ton of stuffed toys. Make a chart of all our stuffed toys below. Liam's chart is done for you.

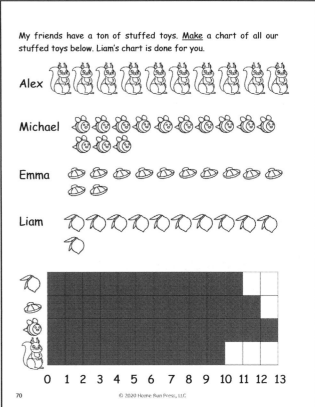

Alex

Michael

Emma

Liam

0 1 2 3 4 5 6 7 8 9 10 11 12 13

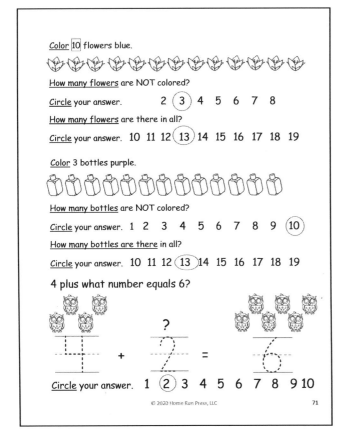

Color 10 flowers blue.

How many flowers are NOT colored?

Circle your answer.   2 ③ 4 5 6 7 8

How many flowers are there in all?

Circle your answer.   10 11 12 ⑬ 14 15 16 17 18 19

Color 3 bottles purple.

How many bottles are NOT colored?

Circle your answer.   1 2 3 4 5 6 7 8 9 ⑩

How many bottles are there in all?

Circle your answer.   10 11 12 ⑬ 14 15 16 17 18 19

4 plus what number equals 6?

4 + 2 = 6

Circle your answer.   1 ② 3 4 5 6 7 8 9 10

Count the objects. Write the number. Add and subtract the objects.

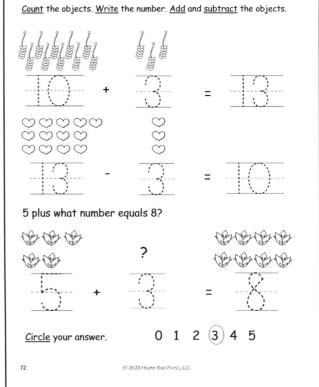

10 + 3 = 13

13 - 3 = 10

5 plus what number equals 8?

5 + 3 = 8

Circle your answer.   0 1 2 ③ 4 5

© 2020 Home Run Press, LLC

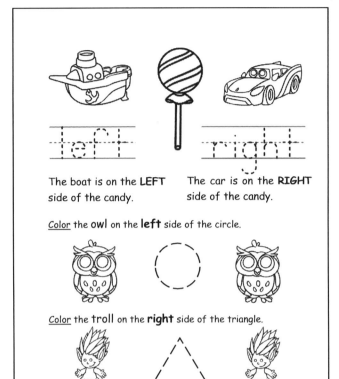

The boat is on the **LEFT** side of the candy.

The car is on the **RIGHT** side of the candy.

<u>Color</u> the owl on the **left** side of the circle.

<u>Color</u> the troll on the **right** side of the triangle.

<u>Say</u> the number. <u>Trace</u> the number. <u>Write</u> the number.

I see 14 butterflies.

14 14 fourteen

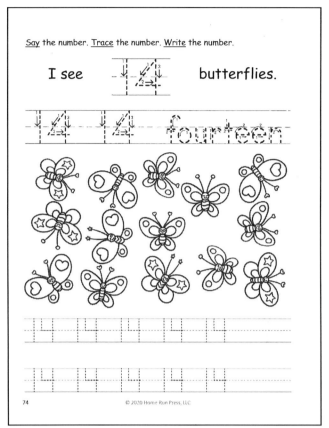

My Grandma baked 2 apple pies. I ate a half of the pies. <u>How many pies</u> are left?

I ate!

<u>Circle</u> your answer:

0 (1) 2 3 4 5

I found 6 shells. My brother broke a half of the shells. <u>How many shells</u> are left?

<u>Circle</u> your answer:

0 1 2 (3) 4 5

I got 4 cupcakes. I ate a half of them. <u>How many cupcakes</u> are left?

<u>Circle</u> your answer:

0 1 (2) 3 4 5

My birthday cake weighed 8 pounds! My friends ate a half of the cake. <u>How many pounds</u> are left?

<u>Circle</u> your answer: 0 1 2 3 (4) 5

<u>Color</u> 10 flowers red.

<u>How many flowers</u> are NOT colored?

<u>Circle</u> your answer.   2 3 (4) 5 6 7 8

<u>How many flowers</u> are there in all?

<u>Circle</u> your answer. 10 11 12 13 (14) 15 16 17 18 19

<u>Color</u> 4 cupcakes brown.

<u>How many cupcakes</u> are NOT colored?

<u>Circle</u> your answer. 1 2 3 4 5 6 7 8 9 (10)

<u>How many cupcakes</u> are there in all?

<u>Circle</u> your answer. 10 11 12 13 (14) 15 16 17 18 19

2 plus what number equals 7?

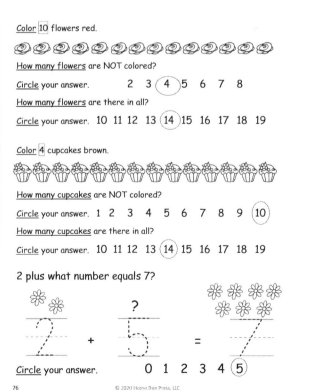

2 + 5 = 7

<u>Circle</u> your answer.   0 1 2 3 4 (5)

Say the word. Trace the word. Write the word. Trace the shapes.

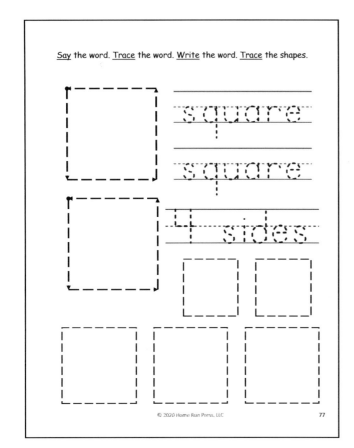

Count the objects. Write the number. Add and subtract the objects.

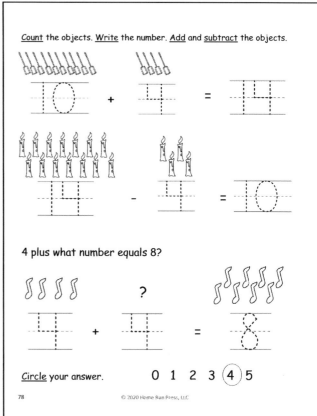

4 plus what number equals 8?

Circle your answer.   0 1 2 3 (4) 5

Say the word. Trace the word. Write the word. Trace the shapes.

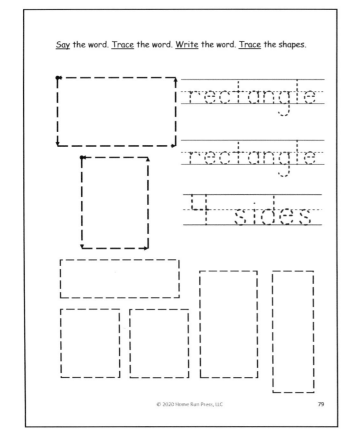

Say the number. Trace the number. Write the number.

I see 15 fruits.

Compare the items. Write the sign (>, <, or =) in the circle. Use >
(greater than), < (less than), or = (equal to).

>

>

>

<

>

<

Color 5 lemons yellow.

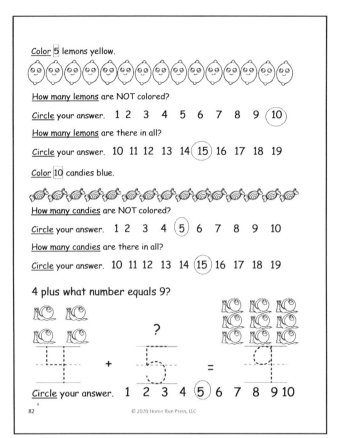

How many lemons are NOT colored?

Circle your answer.   1 2   3   4   5   6   7   8   9 (10)

How many lemons are there in all?

Circle your answer.   10 11 12 13 14 (15) 16 17 18 19

Color 10 candies blue.

How many candies are NOT colored?

Circle your answer.   1 2   3   4 (5) 6   7   8   9   10

How many candies are there in all?

Circle your answer.   10 11 12 13 14 (15) 16 17 18 19

4 plus what number equals 9?

4 + 5 = 9

Circle your answer.   1   2   3   4 (5) 6   7   8   9 10

Count the objects. Write the number. Add and subtract the objects.

10 + 5 = 15

15 - 5 = 10

6 plus what number equals 9?

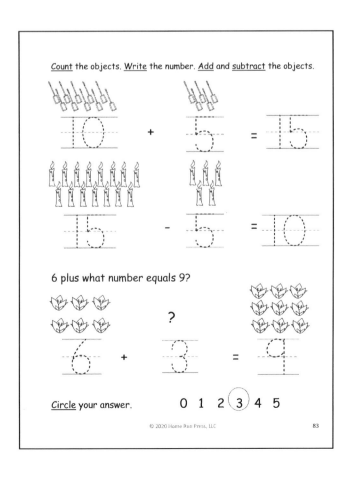

6 + 3 = 9

Circle your answer.   0   1   2 (3) 4   5

Use nickels to measure each toy. Color the tallest toy.

6 nickels   5 nickels

Use nickels to find the price of each toy. Color the cheapest toy.

9 nickels   12 nickels

Say the number. Trace the number. Write the number.

I see ~~16~~ cherries.

16 16 16   sixteen

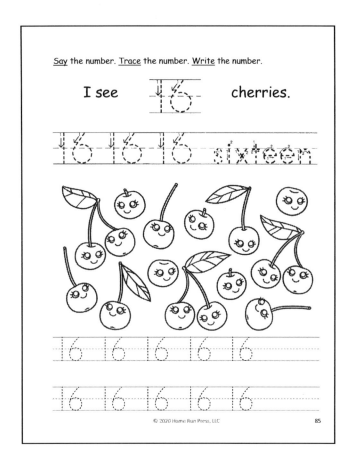

16 16 16 16 16

16 16 16 16 16

Color 6 strawberries red.

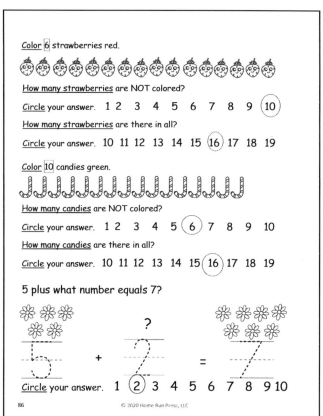

How many strawberries are NOT colored?

Circle your answer.   1 2 3 4 5 6 7 8 9 (10)

How many strawberries are there in all?

Circle your answer.   10 11 12 13 14 15 (16) 17 18 19

Color 10 candies green.

How many candies are NOT colored?

Circle your answer.   1 2 3 4 5 (6) 7 8 9 10

How many candies are there in all?

Circle your answer.   10 11 12 13 14 15 (16) 17 18 19

5 plus what number equals 7?

5 + 2 = 7

Circle your answer.   1 (2) 3 4 5 6 7 8 9 10

I am a number that is smaller than 5 and bigger than 3. What number am I?

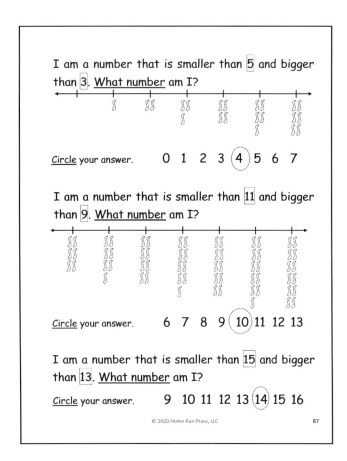

Circle your answer.   0 1 2 3 (4) 5 6 7

I am a number that is smaller than 11 and bigger than 9. What number am I?

Circle your answer.   6 7 8 9 (10) 11 12 13

I am a number that is smaller than 15 and bigger than 13. What number am I?

Circle your answer.   9 10 11 12 13 (14) 15 16

Say the word. Trace the word. Write the word. Trace the shapes.

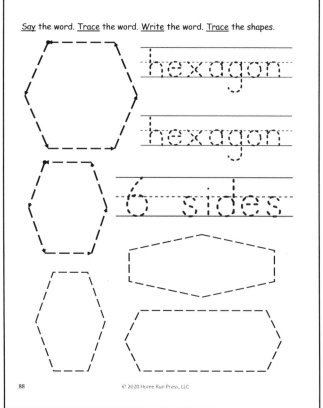

hexagon

hexagon

6 sides

124

Count the objects. Write the number. Add and subtract the objects.

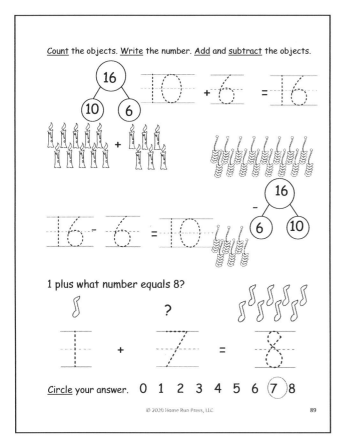

1 plus what number equals 8?

$1 + 7 = 8$

Circle your answer.   0 1 2 3 4 5 6 (7) 8

Say the number. Trace the number. Write the number.

I see 17 cupcakes.

17 17 seventeen

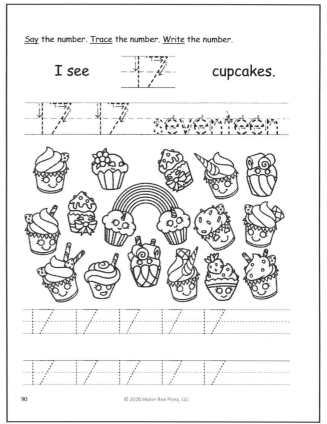

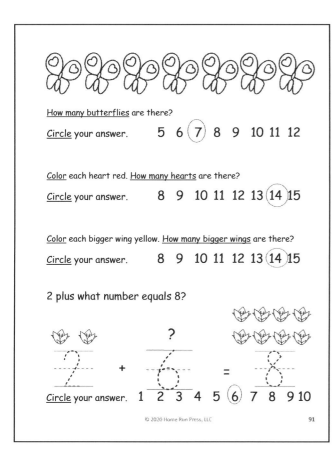

How many butterflies are there?

Circle your answer.   5   6 (7) 8   9   10 11 12

Color each heart red. How many hearts are there?

Circle your answer.   8   9   10 11 12 13 (14) 15

Color each bigger wing yellow. How many bigger wings are there?

Circle your answer.   8   9   10 11 12 13 (14) 15

2 plus what number equals 8?

$2 + 6 = 8$

Circle your answer.   1   2   3   4   5 (6) 7   8   9 10

Use dimes to measure each troll. Color the shortest troll.

6 dimes

5 dimes

Use dimes to find the price of each toy. Color the cheapest toy.

17 dimes   13 dimes

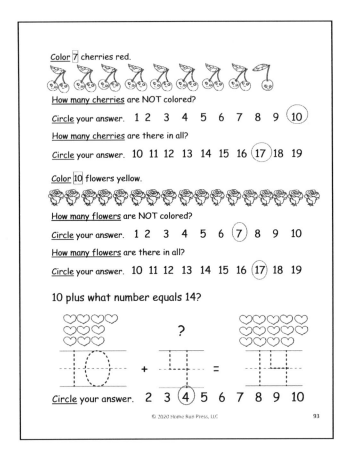

Color **7** cherries red.

How many cherries are NOT colored?

Circle your answer. 1 2 3 4 5 6 7 8 9 (10)

How many cherries are there in all?

Circle your answer. 10 11 12 13 14 15 16 (17) 18 19

Color **10** flowers yellow.

How many flowers are NOT colored?

Circle your answer. 1 2 3 4 5 6 (7) 8 9 10

How many flowers are there in all?

Circle your answer. 10 11 12 13 14 15 16 (17) 18 19

10 plus what number equals 14?

Circle your answer. 2 3 (4) 5 6 7 8 9 10

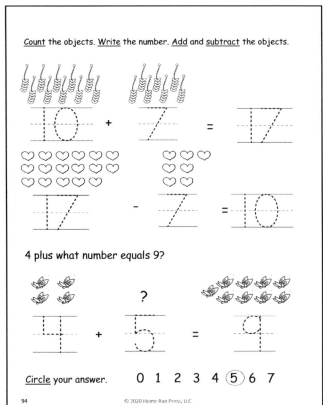

Count the objects. Write the number. Add and subtract the objects.

4 plus what number equals 9?

Circle your answer.   0 1 2 3 4 (5) 6 7

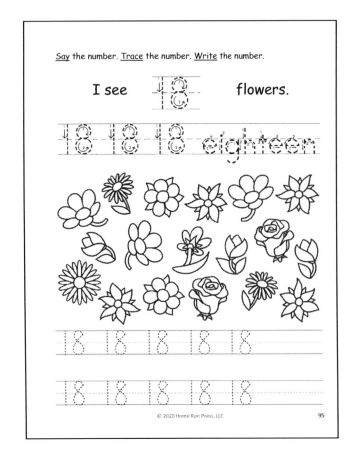

Say the number. Trace the number. Write the number.

I see **18** flowers.

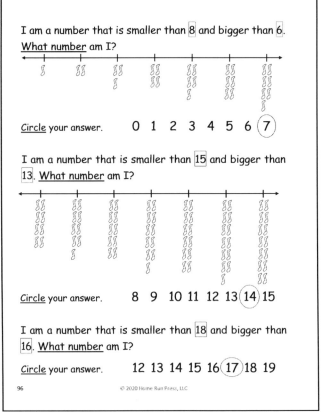

I am a number that is smaller than **8** and bigger than **6**. What number am I?

Circle your answer.   0 1 2 3 4 5 6 (7)

I am a number that is smaller than **15** and bigger than **13**. What number am I?

Circle your answer.   8 9 10 11 12 13 (14) 15

I am a number that is smaller than **18** and bigger than **16**. What number am I?

Circle your answer.   12 13 14 15 16 (17) 18 19

Color 8 cherries.

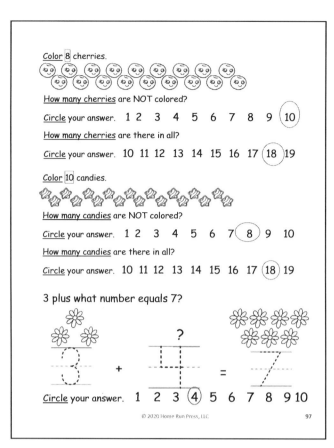

How many cherries are NOT colored?

Circle your answer.   1 2 3 4 5 6 7 8 9 (10)

How many cherries are there in all?

Circle your answer.   10 11 12 13 14 15 16 17 (18) 19

Color 10 candies.

How many candies are NOT colored?

Circle your answer.   1 2 3 4 5 6 7 (8) 9 10

How many candies are there in all?

Circle your answer.   10 11 12 13 14 15 16 17 (18) 19

3 plus what number equals 7?

3 + 4 = 7

Circle your answer.   1 2 3 (4) 5 6 7 8 9 10

Count the objects. Write the number. Add and subtract the objects.

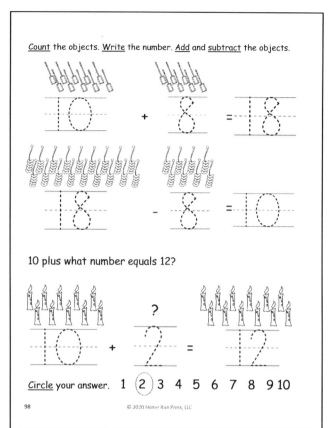

10 + 8 = 18

18 - 8 = 10

10 plus what number equals 12?

10 + 2 = 12

Circle your answer.   1 (2) 3 4 5 6 7 8 9 10

Say the number. Trace the number. Write the number.

I see ___ crayons.

19 19   nineteen

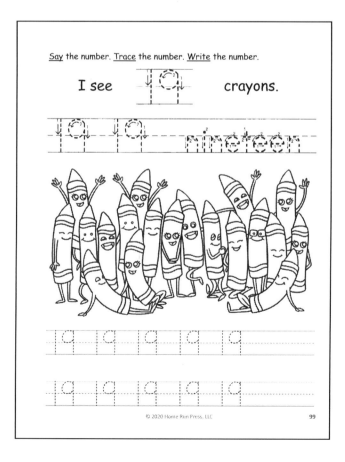

19 19 19 19 19

19 19 19 19 19

Color each star yellow. How many stars are there? ☆

Circle your answer.   5 6 7 8 (9) 10 11 12

Color each Christmas tree ball red. How many balls are there?

Circle your answer.   (8) 9 10 11 12 13 14 15

Color each cloud blue. How many clouds are there? ☁

Circle your answer.   1 2 3 (4) 5 6 7 8

Color the cloud with the **greatest** number in each row.

Color 9 candies green.

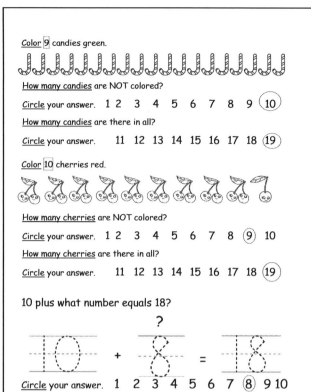

How many candies are NOT colored?

Circle your answer.   1 2 3 4 5 6 7 8 9 (10)

How many candies are there in all?

Circle your answer.   11 12 13 14 15 16 17 18 (19)

Color 10 cherries red.

How many cherries are NOT colored?

Circle your answer.   1 2 3 4 5 6 7 8 (9) 10

How many cherries are there in all?

Circle your answer.   11 12 13 14 15 16 17 18 (19)

10 plus what number equals 18?

?

10 + 8 = 18

Circle your answer.   1 2 3 4 5 6 7 (8) 9 10

Count the objects. Write the number. Add and subtract the objects.

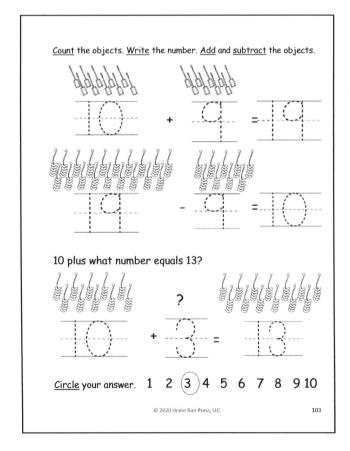

10 + 9 = 19

19 - 9 = 10

10 plus what number equals 13?

?

10 + 3 = 13

Circle your answer.   1 2 (3) 4 5 6 7 8 9 10

Say the number. Trace the number. Write the number.

I see **20** candies.

20 20 twenty

20 20 20 20

20 20 20 20

128

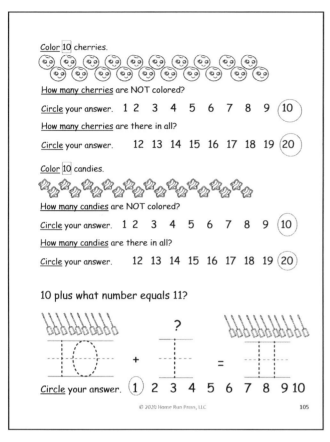

Color 10 cherries.

How many cherries are NOT colored?

Circle your answer.   1 2 3 4 5 6 7 8 9 (10)

How many cherries are there in all?

Circle your answer.   12 13 14 15 16 17 18 19 (20)

Color 10 candies.

How many candies are NOT colored?

Circle your answer.   1 2 3 4 5 6 7 8 9 (10)

How many candies are there in all?

Circle your answer.   12 13 14 15 16 17 18 19 (20)

10 plus what number equals 11?

Circle your answer. (1) 2 3 4 5 6 7 8 9 10

Color the cloud with the **least** number in each row.

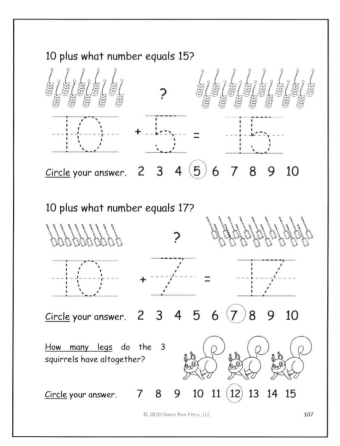

10 plus what number equals 15?

Circle your answer.   2 3 4 (5) 6 7 8 9 10

10 plus what number equals 17?

Circle your answer.   2 3 4 5 6 (7) 8 9 10

How many legs do the 3 squirrels have altogether?

Circle your answer.   7   8   9   10 11 (12) 13 14 15

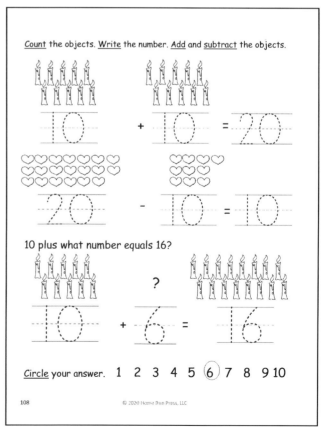

Count the objects. Write the number. Add and subtract the objects.

10 plus what number equals 16?

Circle your answer.   1 2 3 4 5 (6) 7 8 9 10

129

10 plus what number equals 19?

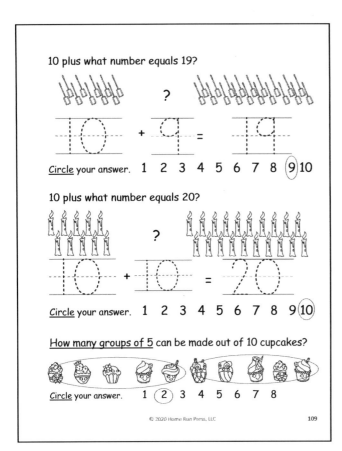

10 + 9 = 19

Circle your answer.   1   2   3   4   5   6   7   8 (9) 10

10 plus what number equals 20?

?

10 + 10 = 20

Circle your answer.   1   2   3   4   5   6   7   8   9 (10)

How many groups of 5 can be made out of 10 cupcakes?

Circle your answer.   1 (2) 3   4   5   6   7   8

Made in the USA
San Bernardino, CA
19 May 2020